PHOBICS AND OTHER PANIC VICTIMS

The Continuum Counseling Series

PHOBICS AND OTHER PANIC VICTIMS

A Practical Guide for Those Who Help Them

Janice N. McLean
and
Sheila A. Knights

Foreword by William Van Ornum
Preface by Arthur B. Hardy, M.D.

Continuum | *New York*

1989

The Continuum Publishing Company
370 Lexington Avenue
New York, NY 10017

Copyright © 1989 by Janice N. McLean and Sheila A. Knights
Foreword Copyright © 1989 by William Van Ornum
Preface Copyright © 1989 by Arthur B. Hardy

Printed in the United States of America

Library of Congress Cataloging-in-Publication Data

McLean, Janice N.
    Phobics and other panic victims : a practical guide for those who
help them / Janice N. McLean and Sheila A. Knights ; foreword by
William Van Ornum ; preface by Arthur B. Hardy.
        p.   cm. — (The Continuum counseling series)
    ISBN 0-8264-0507-X
    1. Phobias.   2. Panic disorders.   I. Knights, Sheila A.
II. Title. III. Series.
RC535.M394   1989
616.85'22506—dc20
                                                            89-32776
                                                            CIP

To Jack, my best everything and greatest advocate.

J. N. M.

To my family and friends who are my support people.

S. A. K.

Author's Note

To protect confidentiality, the names and identifying charac-
teristics of the individuals, couples, and families mentioned in
this book have been changed. Many of the case examples are
composites of several people. Any resemblance to persons living
or dead is entirely coincidental and unintended.

Since making changes in one's life, even positive changes, can
produce anxiety, readers should consult a qualified mental
health professional if any undue anxiety persists.

Contents

Foreword by William Van Ornum, Ph.D.   11

Preface by Arthur B. Hardy, M.D.   15

Acknowledgments   19

Introduction—Helping Those Who Panic: The Victim's Problem, the Family's Problem, the Solution   23

1 | What Are These Disorders and Whom Do They Victimize?: The Panic Package   31

2 | Comprehensive Treatment for Recovery and How to Find It: The Recovery Package   52

3 | How the Spouse (and Family and Friend) Can Help   85

4 | How the Therapist (or Counselor) Can Help   114

5 | How the Physician (or Health Care Professional) Can Help   129

6 | Encouragement and Advice from Support People and Recovered Panic Victims   158

Suggested Readings   169

Bibliography   177

Foreword

The Continuum Counseling Series—the first of its kind for a wide audience—presents books for everyone interested in counseling, bringing to readers practical counseling handbooks that include real-life approaches from current research. The topics deal with issues that are of concern to each of us, our families, friends, acquaintances, or colleagues at work.

General readers, parents, teachers, social workers, psychologists, school counselors, nurses and doctors, pastors, and others in helping fields too numerous to mention will welcome these guidebooks that combine the best professional learnings and common sense, written by practicing counselors with expertise in their specialty.

Increased understandings of ourselves and others is a primary goal of these books—and all professionals agree that greater empathy is the quality essential to effective counseling. Each book offers practical suggestions on how to "talk with" others about the theme of the book—be this in an informal and spontaneous conversation or in a more formal counseling session.

Professional therapists will value these books also, because each volume in The Continuum Counseling Series develops its subject in a unified way, unlike many other books that may be either too technical or as edited collections of papers may come across as being disjointed. In recent years both the American Psychological Association and The American Psychiatric Association have endorsed books that build on the scientific traditions of each profession but are communicated in an interesting way to general readers. We hope that professors and students in fields such as psychology, social work, psychiatry, guidance and counseling, and other helping fields will find these books to be helpful companion readings for undergraduate and graduate courses.

From nonprofessional counselors to professional therapists, from students of psychology to interested lay readers, The Continuum Counseling Series endeavors to provide informative, interesting, and useful tools for everyone who cares about learning and dealing more effectively with these universal, human concerns.

Phobics and Other Panic Victims

In this helpful guidebook, Janice McLean and Sheila Knights offer "support for the support people"—that is, ideas and approaches for people who are important (and often enmeshed) in the lives of people who suffer from panic disorders, including various phobias and agoraphobia. Noting that panic disorder often becomes a family problem, McLean and Knights, both specialists in treating phobias and panic disorder, talk about the impact of this condition on spouses, children, other close family members, and present information that will help all counselors and therapists as well.

Phobics and Other Panic Victims acknowledges that there have been many excellent books written for the victims of the disorder; some of these are even used by therapists who give them to their clients as supplementary readings. What makes this book unique is its focus on the network of persons who interact with the victim of panic disorder. In recent years many stories in the media have brought panic disorder to public attention; some estimates place the number of sufferers in the several millions. Multiply this figure by the individuals within each person's life and we see that this book will be of interest to many.

McLean and Knights examine the thoughts and feelings of both the victims and secondary victims of panic disorder. The role of this latter group is very important, and has been overlooked. They have developed their expertise by working with hundreds of people in "TERRAP" groups, an organization that is devoted to working specifically with victims of panic disorder. They write based on a knowledge of the many detailed ways that panic disorder has an impact:

> You may be the constant chauffeur of the panic victim. You may adjust your vacation plans to meet the safety zone of the victim. You may forego the fun of attending county fairs, sporting events, movies, or any other situation involving crowds of people.

An important theme of the book is that those close to family members can do many things to help the person overcome the disorder. However, there are many ways that assistance can be counterproductive, and in many cases family and friends don't know the right thing to do so they actually help *enable* the panic. McLean and Knights emphasize how to become an advocate, and bring in knowledge from work with alcoholics and their families, as well as stroke victims. Counselors will find this extremely helpful also, as many times they will be seeing someone who knows a victim of panic disorder, and wonder how to react to this sometimes puzzling and perplexing condition.

Counselors who are seeing victims of panic disorder will also learn how to refer them for the specialized help they often need, assistance that can be adjunctive to individual or family therapy.

Another informative section of the book answers typical questions that panic victims ask about treatment. This is written in a helpful, conversational style.

The potential role of medication in working with panic disorder is discussed in an objective and balanced way. There is a chapter specifically devoted to "How the Physician (or Health Care Professional) Can Help." This will illuminate issues not only for helping professionals but will also help spouses, friends, and panic disorder victims themselves better understand what specialized help is available.

Throughout this book there is a theme of hope. Panic disorder is treatable. McLean and Knights have seen many successes in their work, and now they bring their insights to others.

William Van Ornum, Ph.D.
Marist College
Poughkeepsie, New York

General Editor
The Continuum Counseling Series

Preface

It has been my frequent experience that each book published contains one (and sometimes two) worthwhile ideas. It then requires the reader to read the entire book for that worthwhile fact. Finally comes a book that is written for the family, the physician, and the support people who help those suffering from phobias. Every page has worthwhile information valuable to all helpers and sufferers.

The authors have a style that is easy to read, easy to understand, and to the point. It is an excellent book for support people, therapists, and most of all, for the victims of fears, phobias, and panic attack themselves.

The authors' descriptions of the symptoms of panic and the traumatic events precipitating anxiety indicate that much deep thought and consideration of the problem has gone into the preparation of the book. These descriptions of the onset of fears and the expansion of fear come, obviously, from first-hand experiences elicited from numerous patients.

The goals of the book are to provide guidelines for what you have, for why you have it, and what to do about it— and, what is also important, things *not* to do about it. It meets those goals and others.

For the patient, the goal is to let the person know that their condition is treatable provided they can find a comprehensive treatment program run by a specialist in the field who has had training and experience. The authors make clear the likely consequences of "self-treatment" and "no treatment." There is an excellent explanation of the avoidance reactions that cause the expansion of phobias and produce so many of the difficulties. There is recognition of the difficulties, the pitfalls, and the efforts required to get well, and there are copious suggestions for dealing with each stumbling block and pitfall along the road to recovery. The negativity of "what if's" and "WPT" (what people think) with the hidden self-agenda of self-defeating attitudes, are some of the obstacles to overcome on the way to recovery. The authors include several case examples of how to deal with the various adversities in life that are connected with fearfulness.

The book makes the reader realize that this affliction is a "family affair," and a satisfactory recovery requires family help and family participation. There are descriptions of the typical phobic personality, the issues that trigger panic, and perpetuate the "out of nowhere" misconception. It discusses social anxieties, which is a special condition all of its own. It answers commonly asked questions about these disorders and their treatment. It describes the "predisposition theory," the phobic person's "sensitivity," and "catastrophic thinking" that accompanies the fearful state.

In the treatment section, it demonstrates an understanding of the phobic problem that is so insightful that it could have been written by someone who had the experiences him or herself. The authors contrast dead end non-specialist treatment with a comprehensive treatment approach as a guideline for those seeking help and hoping for recovery and not temporary relief by medication. Indeed, it is refreshing to find a book that focuses on multimodal comprehensive treatment rather than merely the physiological theories and chemical treatments for these disorders.

At first I told you that there was a lot of information in

this book, skillfully expressed in words. That is true. It is so full of information that it is hard to put the book down. No one can do it justice in a short preface. It needs to be read and reread.

Phobics and Other Panic Victims not only explains but also offers some "quick fixes" as well as long-term recovery. Definitions are well thought out with real depth and there are numerous meaningful case examples all through the book to enhance the reader's understanding. In the book, there is an excellent, much-needed explanation of advocacy or enhancement.

This book is a must for the phobic, spouse, and family, and it can spell the difference between partial therapy with partial results and comprehensive therapy and recovery. The authors are talented writers, writing on a subject that they thoroughly know.

Arthur B. Hardy, M.D.
Founder, TERRAP Phobia Program,
Past President, Phobia Society
 of America
Member, Board of Directors
 Phobia Society of America

Acknowledgments

First and foremost, we would like to acknowledge the pioneers of anxiety and phobia treatment, Dr. Claire Weekes, Dr. Arthur Hardy, and Dr. Manual Zane, figures who have provided direction, hope, and recovery for millions of panic victims. The expertise these dedicated people have shared through their writings has, we hope, enabled us to continue their model of providing hope and direction to those who are frightened and frustrated by these disorders.

Without the enthusiastic input from the panic victims with whom we have worked, this book would not have met our goals. We thank all of those patients and their support people who patiently and graciously provided us with their input to help others reach the road to recovery. We thank them as well for teaching us to be more helpful with others by learning from their experiences and feedback.

We are extremely grateful to our editorial consultant, Glenna Ann McLean, whose input, expertise, attention to detail and style, and unfailing good humor helped allay "author anxiety." Similarly, without the support, technical assistance, advice, enthusiasm, and humor of John Thornborough, this book would have been less enjoyable to complete.

Thanks are also extended to Continuum Publishing for including our work in their counseling series with special thanks to Bill Van Ornum and Michael Leach for their faith in our ability to reach the goals set for this book.

To Drs. Julian Herskowitz and Steven Lefkowitz, Co-Directors of TERRAP New York, thanks for your support and enthusiasm throughout our involvement with the TERRAP program.

To the family and friends who endured the labor of this endeavor with us, we salute you. Likewise, each author would like to thank the other for the friendship and support that made this book truly a labor of love.

PHOBICS
AND OTHER
PANIC VICTIMS

Introduction
Helping Those Who Panic

The Victim's Problem

It's one of those perfect summer days. White puffs of clouds drift lazily in a bright blue sky. Stretched out on your raft, you savor the fragrance of the ocean breeze. The contrast of hot sun and water's chill is both exhilarating and restful. Eyes closed, you dangle your hand in the water. As friends prepare the afternoon's feast on shore, the scent of fresh sizzled steak wafts out to meet you. You are peaceful, happy, and blissfully alone. . . .

And then you hear it.

"Shark!" And something brushes by your hand.

"Shark!! Shark!!"

A chill speeds up your spine and your heart races. You think, This can't be happening. This is a joke. There is no shark.

You turn your head and see a triangular fin less than a raft's length away. Your skin crawls with a cold, clammy sensation. It's hard to breathe. Why is this happening to me? You try to yell for help or race for shore but you're paralyzed by fear. You know you're powerless to get away and save yourself.

As the fin glides steadily toward you, it's as if you're watching a movie. It can't be real. You can no longer hear the waves, only the sound of your heart beating louder and faster. You want to call for help but realize that no one can help you now. You're trapped. You're sure you're going to die if you don't go crazy first.

All you can do is wait and hope that this terrible menace that has you so totally within its control will leave, taking with it all your fear and paralysis.

Panic. Pure, simple panic. It is logical, understandable. In fact, you would be crazy if you didn't panic. And everyone understands why you panic.

But what about this scene. . . ?

Spring is finally here to stay. You've just hung up the phone having made plans to meet a friend for lunch. As you prepare to leave the house, you feel the exhilaration that comes with pleasant anticipation. The glare of sunshine meets you as you step outside your door. Welcome sounds of spring's first robins and the fragrance of fresh-cut grass fill the air. You feel on top of the world.

A warm breeze blows through your open window as you maneuver the car through familiar streets. The roads are clear of traffic. You're looking forward to the good food and conversation you're about to share. As you slow to a stop for a red light, you're deciding if you should order an appetizer *and* dessert at lunch.

And then you feel it. A chill speeds up your spine and your heart races. You think, What's happening to me? What's wrong?

You try to look around. The road and the car are the same as before, but you are different. Your skin is cold and clammy. You're having trouble breathing. Why is this happening? you ask again. You want to pull over or call out for help, but you're paralyzed by fear. An eternity has gone by and still the light is red. You can no longer hear the car radio, only the sound of your heart beating louder and faster. All of your energy is focused on that light. You're trapped. You're sure you're going to die if you don't go crazy first.

All you can do is wait and hope that this terrible menace that has you so totally within its control will leave, taking with it all your fear and paralysis.

Panic. Pure, simple panic. But there's no logic to it, no understanding. You must be crazy to feel this way. And no one understands. . . .

I am past help, past hope: these are the thoughts of the panic victim. Total fear, total aloneness: these are the feelings of the panic victim.

The Family's Problem

It is late November and you are relaxing in your living room. In the kitchen, your wife is just putting the last of the pies in the oven for the Thanksgiving feast you will host the following day. As you turn to the evening paper's sports section, you notice your wife standing before you, pale, and obviously shaken. In tears, she begs you to take her to the local emergency room; she is having a heart attack.

Suddenly, *you* are pale and obviously shaken. Miraculously managing to control your own panic, you make a dash for the car keys, race to the hospital, and, maddeningly, wait to supply insurance information while your wife is taken to an examining room.

Waiting for word of what is happening, your mind is a jumble of thoughts. You try to remember when you last told her you loved her. You think how terrible life would be without her, and wonder why the two of you have never talked about the possibility of something like this happening. You try desperately to figure out what people do in a situation like this, and wonder how you can possibly control your anxiety enough to remember where the kids are and how to get in touch with them. You can't remember ever feeling so scared, so alone, and so totally unsure of what to do.

Lost in thought, you look up to see your wife and her doctor walking toward you. Your wife, the doctor explains, has *not* had a heart attack. She has simply had a *panic attack*, and she is going to be fine. You don't know whether to laugh first, or cry.

Over the course of the next few days, you find yourself feeling incredibly lucky to have been spared such a catastrophic shift in your life. Everything, after all, is going to be fine. . . .

But then it happens again. Another attack. This time you're sure it's not a heart attack, but your wife pleads with you to check it out just to be safe. But again, you and your wife are sent home from the emergency room with the instructions—"Don't worry, just try to cut down on stress. And, if you feel the need, take one of these pills."

It keeps happening. But now you no longer go for medical help. In fact, you're finding yourself getting a little irritable with your wife and wondering if this is a ploy for attention. You don't know what "stress" she's supposedly reacting to. In fact, you see her life as pretty pressure-free.

By now it's really gotten frustrating. For the last several weeks your wife has refused to go with you to places that are crowded; movies, stores, even to the kid's sports events and concerts. She's lost her sense of humor, too. She's moody, and sometimes you can tell she's been crying. And now she wants you to do the chauffeuring of the kids, and the grocery shopping, but you just don't understand why she can't do it like always. Now the kids are in the middle of the struggle over the driving duties, and the shopping just isn't getting done, and everyone seems unhappy. In fact, there's more tension in your home than you can ever remember. And the anxiety attacks are getting closer and closer together.

What's happening to the woman I married? you ask yourself over and over. Why is this happening to her? And why is this happening to me, and the kids? Can't anything be done to make things the way they used to be? You can't remember ever feeling so scared, so alone, and so totally unsure of what to do.

The Solution

How do panic victims and their families find the comprehensive help they need? Some are lucky. They are referred for specialized treatment by a physician or other professional knowledgeable about the disorder and comprehensive treatment programs for it.

Unfortunately, the majority of panic victims who reach specialized professional help are *self*-referred after a long, lonely, and frustrating search for recovery. Frequently, the victim's search has been ended through "maps" provided not by the physician, or counselor, or family, but through less personal sources: a Phil Donahue show, a *Family Circle* article, a radio talk show, an Ann Landers column, a friend of a friend of a friend. Still, they are the fortunate ones. They connect with the help they need to solve an overwhelming problem.

But what about the victims of panic who don't know where to find help? How about those who are so immobilized by fear that they are unable to reach out for help? And what about the often forgotten *secondary* victims of these disorders; the spouse, the children, the close family, and any other supportive figures who care for and worry about the primary victim? These are the people whose lives, like the life of the primary victim, are also so disrupted. Not *directly* by phobias or panic, but by having to work around these disorders, having to "fill in" for the victim, and having to be understanding of a disorder that they really just *can't* understand!

What about the physician, therapist, friend, pastor, or health care worker in whom the panic victim confides? Where do they turn to best help the victim reach recovery? They (you) turn to this book.

Phobics and Other Panic Victims is directed at you, the confidant of the panic victim—the potential link between the panic victim and comprehensive treatment programs. This book is *not* directed toward the primary panic victim. There are already several excellent books that are supportive of their difficulties. This book is for those people who want their own lives to return to normal by helping to speed the recovery process of the panic victim they know. It is also for the professionals and other helpers who are frustrated in feeling lost about how best to direct the victim to comprehensive help.

Phobics and Other Panic Victims will tell you about the many facets of phobias and panic disorders—symptoms, causes, fears of the victim, associated issues, specifics on how you can help in your own special relationship with the victim, and, most importantly, an overview of comprehensive treatment programs and readings. As such, you will be a very valuable member of the treatment team: someone who can end the panic victim's search for treatment by providing valid direction.

But, while you are appreciated as a pivotal part of the treatment team, it is not our intent to train you in therapeutic techniques. Our goal is to tell you everything you need to know to direct the victim to comprehensive treatment and to support them once they are there. Once the victim is in comprehensive treatment, your role becomes that of offering supplemental support from a position of greater understanding.

This book also serves as a guidebook for the family, friends, and professionals who interact with a victim already in comprehensive treatment. As such, it will "support the support people" by explaining the disorder and the special role you can play in helping the victim (and family!) reach recovery.

Congratulations to you for making this first step toward understanding panic and phobia treatment more fully. Chances are that you have looked long and hard for guidance in understanding these disorders, finding comprehensive treatment sources, and, most importantly, to learn how *you*, personally, can hasten the recovery process. We will help you reach all of those goals.

1

What Are These Disorders and Whom Do They Victimize?: The Panic Package

Panic is a formidable enemy. For every direct panic victim, there are several secondary victims: the spouse or partner, the children, parents, close friends, sometimes even the employer and coworkers. In short, all of the people with whom the panic victim shares his life; all of the people whose own lives are affected by worrying about the victim, and filling in for the victim. It's those people who are asked to be understanding when the victim can't do something promised; a thing like taking a family vacation, attending a son's awards ceremony, or a husband's company dinner dance. These are the secondary, often forgotten, victims of panic and you may be one of them.

If you are a secondary victim of panic, you may be aware of the thoughts, feelings, and behaviors you have in reaction to your husband's or wife's or parent's or friend's disorder. In fact, you may feel a little sheepish about the fact that some of those thoughts aren't so noble ("I don't deserve this blankety-blank hassle in my life!"). And some of your feelings may be a little more negative than you'd like ("I resent that I'm the one doing all the work when *he's* the one with the panic!").

31

By now, the way you "fill in" for, or help your victim with the panic, may have become routine behavior (pick a vacation spot within twelve miles of home, stay by her side in the mall, ask him if he's okay when he gets quiet), and it's beginning to test your patience. So besides getting a first-hand look at how one person's panic can affect a whole series of people, you're also learning that there's a very human side to you.

What Is the Panic Package?

We use the term *panic package* to describe the far-reaching effects of a panic disorder and agoraphobia on not only the direct victim but the secondary victims as well—the family and other support people of the primary sufferer. These disorders don't victimize one person in isolation, but many people in a ripple effect. In fact, in severe cases of these disorders, the "ripple effect" upon the support people may seem more like a tidal wave in the impact it has on the lives of these secondary victims.

Here's a typical example to show just how the panic package works:

* *For the primary victim of panic,* it starts with a fluttery stomach, then, immediately, rapid heartbeat, sweaty palms . . . warmth all over . . . rubbery knees, shakiness, a tightness in the chest . . . then dizziness, a feeling of detachment, unreality, doom. Terror: of an impending heart attack, of losing control, of going crazy. . . .

These are the frightening symptoms, thoughts, and feelings of the panic victim. Whether they are experiencing a panic attack for the first time, or the thousandth time, the experience is just as frightening, just as frustrating. The worry of having a panic attack at any time, any place, without warning, results in a pattern of staying close to a "safe person"—a person who can be counted upon to help them in case of panic. It results in a pattern of avoiding places from which escape is difficult or delayed. It results in avoidance of social situations in which they might be scrutinized by others in the event of panic.

This avoidance is logical in a way, but in practice, the victims become prisoners of their own "what ifs." For example, "What if I panic while driving?" (I'll drive off the bridge!) "What if I panic in the mall?" (I'll lose control and go screaming out of the store!) "What if I lose control at the party?" (I'll humiliate myself forever!).

What is the victim's solution to fighting these fears? Simple—avoid any situation that might trigger such fears. Avoid any situations involving separation from a safe person. Avoid any situations involving delayed escape from public places. Avoid any social situations. In short, the victim develops his own set of commandments for minimizing the fear of losing control:

Don't drive alone
Don't travel too far from home
Don't go into situations involving crowds
Don't go into grocery stores
Don't go to shopping malls
Don't go to church
Don't go to movies
Don't go to parties
Don't eat in restaurants
Don't fly in airplanes

Of course, many panic victims are not at such a severe stage of avoidance. While they may enter into all of these situations, nevertheless, they do so with a tremendous amount of anxiety. Panic victims within this group of people have the same commandments, but add a simple qualifier: "without feeling very anxious." Therefore, their commandments are as follows:

Don't drive alone without feeling very
   anxious
Don't travel too far from home without feeling very anxious
Don't go into situations involving crowds without feeling
   very anxious
Don't go into grocery stores without feeling very anxious

. . . and so on.

If you are a secondary panic victim, chances are that you have had to make some very significant changes in your own life to help your panic victim with his or her disorder. Think about it. For each of the commandments the panic victim has, there is someone, possibly you, who is called into play to enforce that commandment.

For example, let's take the first commandment of the panic victim: Don't drive, or in less severe cases, don't drive without feeling very anxious. Who is called upon to do the driving for the panic sufferer who does not drive? You! And who is called upon to be the safe person in supporting the nervous driver whose commandment is "Don't drive without feeling very anxious?" You! Refer back to those commandments lists for a moment or two. Take a look at the effect those commandments have on the lives of the support people, usually the spouse, children, and parents of the panic victim.

Who does the grocery shopping for the wife who can't? Who attends the children's open school nights alone? You know the routine if you have lived with a panic victim for a while. And you know who usually "fills in" for the immobilized victim, or who adjusts his schedule to accompany the victim in each of the situations outlined. You do.

You may be the constant chauffeur of the panic victim. You may adjust your vacation plans to meet the safety zone of the victim. You may forego the fun of attending county fairs, sporting events, movies, or any other situation involving crowds of people. You may give up eating at your favorite restaurant, or feel so anxious yourself about having to leave suddenly that you can't enjoy your meal. You may do the grocery shopping alone, or starve! You may go to parties by yourself or miss them altogether, and it's difficult deciding which is harder. In fact, you may become an expert at making excuses why you must miss yet another party, wedding, or other event you wanted so much to attend.

Now who is the victim of panic? Everyone—the primary victim and his or her support system. Each and every victim succumbs to a predictable combination of thoughts, feelings, and behaviors in response to the disorder.

The Thoughts, Feelings, and Behavior of the Primary Victim

For primary panic victims, the *thoughts* that they have about their disorder usually fuel the strength of the disorder. Panic victims are known for their ability to use their vivid imaginations to frighten themselves, rather than to calm themselves down. Dr. Arthur Hardy, director of the TERRAP Phobia Program, calls these thoughts "what if" statements. Here are some examples:

What if I have a heart attack?
What if I panic in a store full of people and make a fool of myself?
What if I go out by myself and feel faint—who will help me?
What if I need to use the bathroom and can't find one in time?

The primary victim's *feelings* are emotional responses to their thoughts about the disorder. The most common ones are fear and embarrassment: the fear of having further attacks and the embarrassment of having others find out. Both of these feelings can keep people locked into the disorder. Here are other feeling statements:

I feel *angry* with myself because I can't stop the phobia on my own.

I'm *worried* that these attacks will happen again while I'm alone.

I feel *guilty* because I can't do things or go places with my kids.

I'm *nervous* that people will reject me if I tell them about my disorder.

The *behavior* of the primary victim reflects an attempt to cope with these unsettling thoughts and feelings about the disorder. Here are examples:

I sit near the door in restaurants and near exits in movie theaters so I can run out if I need to.

I buy only four or five things at a time so I don't feel trapped in the supermarket.

I tell people that I don't have my driver's license so I'm not expected to carpool the children.

I go shopping only with my husband and my mother.

The Thoughts, Feelings, and Behavior of the Secondary Victims

The *thoughts* the secondary victims have about the disorder and about the direct victim determine how they feel toward and behave with that victim. Such thoughts can be supportive, critical, or, more likely, a mixture of the two. Here are examples:

She needs me to do so many things. Who will take care of her if I get sick?

I have to be careful of what I say to him or I might trigger an attack.

This panic stuff is so childish!

I'm tired of always being the one to go grocery shopping.

The *feelings* of the secondary victims reflect both the supportive and critical thoughts they have about the disorder and its effect on the primary victim. Usually, this mixture of thoughts results in a combination of feelings about the disorder. Here are examples:

I feel *helpless* and *scared* when he has a panic attack.

I feel *frustrated* in having to do things alone that should be family activities.

I feel *angry* because she doesn't seem to be willing to do something about her problem.

I feel *happy* to be so needed.

The *behavior* of the secondary victims usually involves taking on duties the victim cannot perform. It also reflects making significant changes in their individual life-styles to accommodate the limitations of the direct victim. Here are examples:

I have to do all the shopping; for food, clothes, and anything else we need.

I had to stop taking night courses for my college degree so that my wife wasn't home alone.

We spend all of our vacations in our backyard.

I've taken over the finances because he is so anxious he can't sit down long enough to fill out the paperwork.

At this point, you should appreciate the fact that panic is not a simple disorder that affects one individual, but rather a package of thoughts, feelings, and behaviors involving both direct and secondary victims. For every *thought* the primary victim has about the disorder, (I can't stand being so disabled!), the husband or child or parent has thoughts about the disorder (If only she weren't so dependent on me!). For every negative *feeling* the victim has (I feel guilty that I can't attend my son's school play!), the family member also has strong feelings (If my mother *really* cared about me, she'd come to my play!). And for every *behavior* change the victim makes in response to the disorder (avoiding grocery shopping to prevent panic), there is behavioral change in the victim's family (taking on the job of grocery shopping).

In clinical settings, recognizing this victimization of those beyond the primary victim is called a *systems approach*. Here, we might simply say that a panic disorder is a family affair. Given the fact that panic disorders significantly affect both the direct victim and the family and support people, two things become obvious:

1. The primary victim owes it to these others as well as himself or herself to seek comprehensive treatment.
2. Recovery from these disorders is based upon an understanding of the disorder by the family as well as the victim, cooperating with comprehensive treatment, and making the necessary changes in behavior to hasten the recovery process. Therefore, while the primary victim of panic is the main focus of comprehensive treatment, these secondary victims must also be addressed to understand and change the system within which the panic thrives.

Let's begin with understanding these disorders; what we know about their development, comprehensive treatment, and how you personally can help the primary victim. As a secondary victim, you'll be helping yourself as well.

Who Is Most Likely to Experience a Panic Attack?

Researchers in this field are unable to predict with certainty who will and who won't develop panic attacks leading to such disorders as panic disorder with or without agoraphobia. However, treatment experts such as Hardy, Zane, Weekes, Goldstein, and McCullough see a particular personality type as especially susceptible to the development of panic and the avoidance of panic-inducing situations. Based upon the work of such experts, and our own experience with panic victims, we look at the development of such disorders within a recipe paradigm. It goes like this:

An individual with a certain personality and a certain personal history is likely to develop such disorders under certain circumstances.

Confused? Let's fill in some information to make the recipe more understandable:

Take a Certain Personality Type (several or all of the following):

a people pleaser
a worrier
overly responsible
bottles up feelings
never really feels "grown-up"
superstitious
sees things as black and white

perfectionistic
reacts strongly to mild stimuli
overly sensitive to criticism
tends to take on the problems of others
laughs or cries easily
overly affected by tragic headlines
sees self as "just adequate" as a person
very concerned about what others will think
overly conscientious at work and parenting
tries very hard to be "good"
has a strong sense of right, wrong, and fairness

Add a Certain Type of Personal History (two or more of the following):

loss of a parent or parental figure through death or perceived abandonment
sudden loss of support or a change in an important inter-
personal relationship
difficulty separating from family: school phobias, sleep-
overs with friends, college homesickness
physical, sexual, and/or emotional abuse as a child
overattachment to a parent or parents
parental history of alcoholism
taught to bottle up feelings
childhood exposure to a yeller or screamer on a regular
basis
childhood exposure to a worrier on a regular basis
childhood exposure to an overly demanding authority figure
other traumatic events in childhood and early adulthood

Expose to One or More of the Following Events or Adjustments in Early Adulthood (usually in the person's twenties or thirties):

death of a significant figure in the person's life
sudden loss or disruption of an important relationship

birth of a child
hospitalization resulting in dependency upon others
an argument with a significant figure in the person's life
negative criticism from an authority figure
going away to college
entrapment in a physically or emotionally abusive relationship
a switching of gears from career to homemaking
divorce or separation
ongoing physical illness
perceived betrayal by a significant figure
a specific traumatic event: accident, physical assault, rape
loss of a significant relationship through argument, moving, breakup, etc.
social isolation due to geographical area, lack of friends, etc.

Yield: A Person Likely to Experience a Panic Attack

What Is a Panic Attack?

1. The victim of a panic attack experiences at least four of the following symptoms: the sudden onset of intense apprehension, fear, or terror; a feeling of impending doom; shortness of breath, or a smothering feeling; dizziness; heart palpitations or rapid heart rate; shaking or trembling; numbness or a tingling sensation; chest pain or discomfort; feelings of depersonalization or unreality; sweating, nausea, or intestinal distress; a choking sensation; chills or hot flashes; and a fear of dying, going crazy, or losing control during the attack and doing something impulsive and embarrassing.
2. As if this weren't enough, the victim experiences these symptoms unexpectedly, or out of the blue, and therefore with no warning to permit preparation. There is no clear reason for this transformation—the victim

might be picnicking with good friends, relaxing at home, or standing on line at the bank when the attack occurs.

3. Finally, these attacks are not the result of any organic disorders that could generate such symptoms, such as thyroid irregularities, caffeine intoxication, or amphetamine use.

For those readers who have suffered a panic attack, no further description of this frightening experience is necessary. For those who have not, simply reading the previous description of the physical symptoms, thoughts, and feelings comprising the panic attack should give you an intellectual appreciation for the panic victim you know. But what about the feelings and sensations part of it? How can you understand something you're never experienced? The answer, of course, is that you really *can't* understand it fully unless you have experienced such an episode. Just as those of us who have never been prisoners of war can never fully appreciate the torment and aftermath of such an experience, so are we unable to fully understand and sympathize with the torment of the panic victim. This is one of the most frustrating parts of having such attacks—the inability of others to understand what you are experiencing and the types of thoughts, feelings, and behaviors that you develop in reaction to such panic attacks.

This is why, in working with the spouse and family of panic victims, it is so important to explain the panic experience within a context that "hits home" for those support people. While you, the reader, may be lucky enough to have never experienced panic, consider the physical reactions, thoughts, and feelings you would expect to have in the following situations:

1. You return home from work one evening to find several ambulances and police cars in your driveway—all with sirens wailing and lights flashing.

2. While making a hairpin turn on a winding mountain road, you feel your car begin to skid, and realize there is no way to stop it from sliding over the cliff.
3. You answer your doorbell late one night to find three men with masks and guns shoving you back into the house while shouting obscenities.

It's unpleasant to even *think* about such situations, isn't it? Now imagine experiencing your reaction to these situations over and over again, but without understanding why you were undergoing such a dramatic transformation, without the comfort of being able to say to yourself, "Well, of course I'm terrified—look what's going on!" This is the life of the panic victim.

What Is Panic Disorder?

The Diagnostic and Statistical Manual of Mental Disorders (DSM-III-R), refers to this disorder as Panic Disorder without Agoraphobia. Here, while the victim suffers recurrent panic attacks, this has little or no effect on that victim's social or occupational functioning. In other words, the victim suffers the attacks, but shows little or no avoidance of situations or settings from which escape might be difficult or delayed. The large majority of people with Panic Disorder *do* begin to avoid such situations, however, and, in such cases, the disorder usually progresses to Panic Disorder with Agoraphobia.

What Is Panic Disorder with Agoraphobia?

This disorder meets the criteria of panic disorder, but the victim has also developed a fear of being in situations or places from which escape might be difficult or embarrassing if he or she begins to panic. Examples of such settings would be the use of public transportation, driving, standing in line, grocery stores, situations involving crowds, shopping malls, or being on a bridge. There is also usually a fear that help might not be available if a panic attack should occur in one of these settings. As a result of these fears, the person either needs a trusted companion when away from home, or the person restricts travel. There are three levels of agoraphobic avoidance:

Mild: Here, the victim shows only minimal avoidance in his or her daily activities. Such individuals might travel unescorted to work or shopping, but otherwise avoid traveling alone. A mild level is also seen in people who enter all difficult situations, but do so with distress. Most victims of mild agoraphobia live a relatively normal life-style.

Moderate: Here, the person's degree of avoidance results in a restrictive life-style. In such cases, the victim is able to leave the house alone, but limits travel to within a few miles of home unless accompanied by a trusted companion.

Severe: Here, the person's pattern of avoidance results in an inability to leave the house at all, or only in the company of a trusted companion. Sadly, while the life-style of the severe agoraphobic is the most restricted, the difficulty of leaving home is often an obstacle in reaching the comprehensive treatment this very needy person requires.

What Is Agoraphobia without History of Panic Disorder?

In this relatively rare disorder, as its name implies, the victim is agoraphobic, but has no history of panic disorder. Here, while the person avoids situations from which escape could be difficult or embarrassing, it is from the fear of experiencing only selected symptoms of the panic attack. Since the person has never experienced a full panic disorder, the fear is largely that of "What if my limited attack develops into a full-blown panic attack?" This anticipatory anxiety maintains a pattern of avoidance.

What Is Social Phobia?

Individuals with this disorder experience excessive and unreasonable anxiety in social situations where they are exposed to the scrutiny of others. The major fear here is not primarily of having a panic attack that could result in embarrassment, as with agoraphobia, but a fear of *acting* in a way that would be humiliating or embarrassing independently of a panic attack. Specific fears of the social phobic range from fear or speaking in public or choking on food while eating in front of others, to an inability to urinate in public rest rooms or trembling while writing in public. Therefore, social phobics avoid—or endure with significant distress—parties, speeches, or any other situation where they could be a focus of someone's attention.

Social phobia is diagnosed only if the avoidance of such situations of possible scrutiny interferes with job functioning, usual social activities, relationships with others, or if there is significant distress about having this fear. This diagnosis does not apply to someone who fears public scrutiny due to another disorder such as stuttering or the trembling of Parkinson's disease.

What Is a Simple Phobia?

Simple phobias are also referred to as specific phobias. Here, the object of fear and excessive anxiety is of a specific object or situation, rather than the fear of having a panic attack or suffering the scrutiny of others. Simple phobias are rather common in the general population and include the fear of cats, dogs, snakes, mice, insects, closed spaces like elevators, exposure to blood or tissue injuries, heights, and airplane travel. Most people seek treatment for simple phobias only when they significantly interfere with daily functioning. Accordingly, the elevator phobic transferred to a Manhattan skyscraper is more likely to seek treatment than the homemaker who only occasionally encounters an elevator, and even then can use the stairway.

Now that the disorders involving panic have been defined, let's identify and answer the most common questions the panic victim has about these disorders.

1. How Does Anxiety Differ From Panic?

Anxiety symptoms are uncomfortable, but manageable; you can continue in your normal daily activities even while manifesting anxiety symptoms: dry mouth, stomach butterflies, shortness of breath. Indeed, there are times when a little anxiety is even good for us. Anxiety related to an upcoming exam spurs us to study a little harder. Anxiety about a job interview causes us to get a shoeshine or practice our handshake. Anxiety can sometimes give us that little edge we need to improve our performance.

The feeling of panic seems to come out of the blue. It doesn't seem to be related to present activities. It lasts for discrete periods of time, departing as suddenly as it arrived, and there is a sharp rise then an abrupt fall in the physical symptoms. While anxiety can last for days, it usually stays within manageable levels. Panic's intensity is self-limiting since the body cannot maintain that state of intensity for prolonged periods of time.

2. Could I Have a Heart Attack or Die From a Panic Attack?

The answer is no. While the panic attack gives you physical symptoms, it is not connected to any medical condition and does not show any damage to the systems involved in a panic attack when medical tests are run during the attack. Of course, we recommend that you consult a physician to rule out any possible physical factors or medical conditions involved in your anxiety and panic. (Examples are thyroid irregularities and caffeine intoxication.) Your physician can also allay your worry by telling you under what circumstances your symptoms should be medically evaluated to rule out physical involvement.

3. Can I Totally Lose Control during a Panic Attack?

No! This is a common fear and one that keeps many panic victims from even attempting activities they fear might bring on a panic attack. Although most panic victims fear this total loss of control, most are unable to clearly define what they mean by "losing control." The general fear is of somehow "losing it" during an attack, and acting so dramatically that the victim is publicly humiliated forever. It is comforting to remember that, despite the panic victim's certainty that "everyone" can immediately detect a panic state, even panic disorder specialists have difficulty recognizing when a victim is experiencing a panic attack. The outward appearance of the victim appears normal to even the trained eye.

4. How Long Does a Panic Attack Usually Last?

During a panic attack, your sense of time passing is lost and the attack seems to be never-ending. In reality, it usually lasts for only a few minutes. The body cannot sustain the intensity of the panic state for very long and will move to balance itself and relieve the panicky feeling. In rare cases, the panic continues for a longer period of time. However, comprehensive treatment teaches the victim to prevent anxiety from building to this level.

5. How Can I Control My Panic Attack?

Dr. Claire Weekes, in her book *Peace From Nervous Suffering* (1983), tells the reader to "float through" the panic rather than fight it. Like a swimmer caught in a strong current, if you fight the current, you exhaust yourself and are overwhelmed. If you ride the current, you eventually drift onto the shore. This is one of many coping strategies that panic victims learn in comprehensive treatment.

6. Is There a Relationship between Panic Attacks and Inner Ear Disturbances, Mitral Valve Prolapse, and Hypoglycemia?

Although all of these disorders have been explored as possible generators of panic, in fact, statistics indicate that none of these medical conditions occur more frequently in phobia and panic victims than they do in the general public (Goldstein and Stainback, 1987; Sheehan, 1983.)

7. Are Panic Disorders and Phobias Hereditary? Can I Pass Them on to My Children?

Currently, research conducted on this question is inconclusive. While anxiety disorders may appear to "run" in families, it is unclear whether this is due to *heredity* or whether it is *learned behavior* (environment).

Put more simply, the question is, are you *born* with these disorders, or taught to react to life in such a way that you *develop* these disorders? For example, does an anxious and panicky mother unknowingly, by her example, "teach" her children to be anxious, or are those children born anxious? Another question of research interest is a cross between the previous two: are some people born with a *predisposition*, or the tendency to develop such a disorder under a certain set of circumstances? And what are those circumstances?

Confusing the picture are certain facts: some people with these disorders have no known family history of such a disorder, and many anxious and panic-ridden parents have children who are easygoing and free from anxiety. Researchers continue to address this fascinating area with current research leaning toward the predisposition theory.

8. What Do I Tell My Children about My Disorder?

The truth! Often phobics and panic sufferers try to hide their disorder from their children. This is unfair to both parties. Panic victims feel guilty over missing family occasions as well as fearful that the children will reject them for their "tragic flaw." The children are well aware that there is something wrong and may become resentful that no one is telling them the truth, or (perhaps worse) "play along" with the parent and pretend that everything is fine since this seems to be what makes the parent happy.

Children are very sensitive. In an alcoholic family, children as young as four or five are able to recognize that there is something wrong when the parent drinks, but may take the responsibility for that action upon themselves: "I must have been bad. That's why Daddy got drunk and hit me."

Remember that how you tell your children and people in general will determine how they react. Think of the buildup that television soap operas give before a dramatic scene. They can make the common cold seem like a terminal illness. When you talk about phobias and panic attacks, the way you present it is the way it will be perceived. Make the discussion of your disorder matter-of-fact like a story for the newspaper rather than for a tragic novel.

When children are made aware of a situation, they can

deal with it much more capably than we generally assume. It is *not knowing* what is being covered up or lied about that is frightening to them. Children will love and accept us, even with our flaws or vulnerabilities when they are allowed to share in the problem.

Talking about your disorder with your children will not only help them to understand you better, and alleviate their fears about "something" being wrong, but also help them to understand that you are missing family activities *because you are phobic, not because you don't love them.*

Children benefit from good role models—people who can communicate openly and share good coping strategies. By being honest about your disorder and your pursuit of comprehensive treatment, you also teach your children that it is okay to have areas of difficulty, and that those areas can be improved with effort. A comprehensive treatment program will help you in explaining your disorder to your children.

You should now have a good, basic understanding of disorders of panic and their far-reaching effects—the panic package. The next logical question, and perhaps the most important of all is:

9. What Is the First Step toward Recovery?

Whether the panic victim has had the disorder for only months or for several years, recovery is possible. The first step to recovery is in the victim's acceptance of certain facts. Here they are:

There is a name for what is happening to you.
You are not going crazy.
You are not alone. One out of six Americans is victimized by an anxiety disorder, and panic disorder is the most common disorder among those seeking treatment.

There is effective, comprehensive treatment for the disorder.
With determination and hard work, comprehensive treatment can help you reach recovery.

As the secondary victim, or the concerned professional or friend, you can help the primary victim take this first step if he or she hasn't already. Your message is simple: panic, the formidable enemy, can be conquered, and you are there to help.

2

Comprehensive Treatment for Recovery and How to Find It: The Recovery Package

I thought I was dying!
I was sure I was going crazy!
I was terrified I would lose control!
I knew nobody else in the world felt like this!

As panic disorder and phobia specialists, we hear these statements over and over again. Often, panic victims have known fear for a long time before finding help: fear of the symptoms of their disorder, fear that they are "going crazy," or dying, and fear that the panic will last for a lifetime.

The relief these victims experience when connecting with comprehensive treatment is tremendous. The fears and secret thoughts and self-doubts they have been carrying, often for years, are finally unloaded. They are reassured that there is a name for their disorder, that they are not crazy, or doomed, that the disorder is treatable, and that recovery is within their reach. Upon hearing this, they cry, they may laugh nervously, and always they thank you repeatedly for illuminating a light at the end of their tunnel of fears. Then they roll up their sleeves and work toward recovery.

What is frustrating is that this scenario is often the exception rather than the rule. While anxiety disorders now plague the general public more than any other emotional disorder, thousands of victims suffer needlessly simply because they don't know that comprehensive help is available and where to find that help. Therefore, the panic victim becomes overwhelmed by the disorder.

As a support person or professional with access to the panic victim, you have the power to set that victim on the fastest road to recovery by understanding the steps they must follow.

Step One: Avoid Dead Ends to Comprehensive Treatment

Dead End One: The Medication-Only Route

Because panic victims usually assume a medical reason for their anxiety, they make rounds of several physicians investigating all body systems as possible generators of the panic. Indeed, it makes good sense to explore any physical reasons for the panic, and we recommend medical evaluation to rule out the presence of any condition that could generate such symptoms.

However, following exhaustive testing, the vast majority of panic victims are reassured that they are "fine." While this news is reassuring in some respects, in others, it is frightening to the victims. They know that they are, in fact, *not* fine, that something is *very* wrong, and that they surely *must* be crazy to generate such symptoms.

"Reassured" that they are reacting to stress, "nerves," boredom, change of life, midlife crisis, or empty nest syndrome, victims are given well-intentioned, but frustrating advice: pursue a hobby, get a job, make your husband take you out to dinner more often, "relax," or "don't take life so seriously!" Such platitudes can be maddening to a victim since he or she is usually just the person who *never* fully relaxes, doesn't know *how* to take it easy, and has the very logical fear of reacting to some very startling body sensations.

Although the victim's physician is a competent and compassionate professional, he or she may have only a basic knowledge of panic disorder or agoraphobia. Many physicians are unable even to identify these disorders simply because their medical training has not emphasized panic disorders and phobias, or because the patient has not enabled the physician to see the complete clinical picture. Even if the physician is able specifically to diagnose the disorder, he or she is often unaware of the comprehensive program of treatment for such disorders and where it can be found.

This is where the victim enters a dead end to recovery. He or she is prescribed a tranquilizer or other medication to help with the anxiety. However, while medication can be helpful for temporary relief or reduction of anxiety, used in isolation, it is not the course to full recovery. Even with medication, anxiety and panic can occur, resulting in continued difficulty with driving, being alone, or entering public situations. Subsequently, convinced that there is no other or more comprehensive treatment for anxiety, the panic victim is left feeling frustrated, fearful of developing a dependency on medication, and just plain scared of a future filled with panic.

Dead End Two: The Secret Victim Route

A different, equally common background of the panic victim is the following: frightened by the sudden onset of panic attacks, fears fueled by low self-esteem and a poor support system, the victim suffers alone with the panic. He or she is afraid to reach out to any possible sources of help—physicians, therapists, counselors, friends, or even family. Certain that he or she is crazy, different, and experiencing something that no one would understand, and all would ridicule, the victim wears a mask of normalcy while keeping that "terrible secret." Vivid images of being teased, losing control, and humiliating oneself haunt the victim. And the anticipation of being abandoned by family and friends if they knew of these symptoms strengthen the victim's determination to keep them secret. As a result, the victim is left feeling lonely and depressed from the sense of doom, apprehension, and isolation experienced on a daily basis.

Dead End Three: The Nonspecialist Route

A third scenario seen with panic victims seeking help is almost as frustrating. Reassured by their physicians that their disorder is emotional in nature, the victims seek help in a somewhat helpful, but less-effective way: through contact with a professional therapist who is not a specialist in panic disorders and phobias, or through a supportive counselor, clergy, or family friend. Although having the best of intentions, these figures may not be familiar with the disorder the victims present them with, let alone the most comprehensive treatment for recovery. And while the support and insight the victims develop through such sources may be helpful, they are still unable to carry out daily activities without fear. Therefore, the victims are at another dead end, one in which they share the secret and the fears, but to someone who is as unaware as they are about the best route to recovery.

Clearly, all three of these dead ends to recovery have a common outcome: the victim continues to be ignorant of the specifics of the disorder and the route to comprehensive treatment.

Step Two: Be Aware of the Most Comprehensive Treatment for Recovery

Experts in the field of panic and phobia disorders agree that the *most effective* treatment for these disorders is a *package* or *combination* of behavior therapy, education about the disorder, peer group support, cognitive therapy, and medication as appropriate. This is the standard comprehensive treatment program offered by teaching hospitals, universities, and such nationally known treatment centers as the White Plains Hospital Phobia Clinic (White Plains, New York), The Terrap Phobia Program (Menlo Park, California), Roundhouse Square Psychiatric Center (Alexandria, Virginia), and Temple University Agoraphobia and Anxiety Center (Bala Cynwyd, Pennsylvania). Such programs are usually staffed with psychologists, psychiatrists, social workers, and other mental health professionals. Many also utilize recovered panic patients to serve as role models for victims entering a treatment program.

As the package of recovery methods may appear rather vague to the layperson, let's be more specific about what the panic victim could expect to be offered through comprehensive treatment.

The best comprehensive treatment programs include the following components:

1. *Time-limited treatment groups* (usually eight to sixteen weeks) which meet weekly
2. *Instruction in anxiety disorders and the reduction of anxiety* (instruction in the measurement and recording of

symptoms, relaxation training, stress reduction training, cognitive coping strategies, written materials)

3. *In vivo, systematic desensitization sessions*—sessions where a staff member accompanies the patient in entering difficult situations in a step-by-step way (for example, grocery stores, driving, staying alone, separating in a mall, standing in lines, using elevators, crossing bridges)

4. *Evaluation for medication* as appropriate by an affiliated psychiatrist

5. *Instruction in and discussion of related issues of importance* (for panic patients: assertiveness, unresolved grief, anger, incomplete individuation, self-esteem, perfectionism, rigidity of thinking, pessimism, feelings of powerlessness)

6. *An informational session conducted for the family and close support people of the panic victim* providing clarity about the disorder and their role in helping the victim

7. *Journal keeping* (documentation of thoughts, feelings, behavior, practice sessions, progress, and setbacks) that provides insight to the patient and patient monitoring for the therapist

8. *Homework assignments* (readings both directly and indirectly related to the disorder, for example, self-help books, assertiveness readings, practice assignments for extending limits with a practice partner)

9. *Individual psychotherapy and follow-up support groups* as needed to address individual issues and to enhance recovery

This list of treatment components is especially helpful in determining the comprehensiveness of a program a panic victim is considering. The candidates for such treatment should feel comfortable asking any potential therapist or treatment center which treatment components are offered in their program of recovery.

Step Three: Locate a Program of Comprehensive Treatment

There are basically two ways of accomplishing this:

1. Contact the Phobia Society of America to locate the panic disorder and phobia specialists in your vicinity.

2. Contact the national office of the TERRAP Phobia Program to locate a TERRAP therapist in your vicinity.

1. The Phobia Society of America (PSA)

This national, nonprofit organization was founded by phobia specialists, panic and phobia victims, and their families. A primary goal of PSA is to educate the public to the problems, treatment, and research pertaining to disorders of panic. Additionally, the PSA supports victims of these disorders by directing them to treatment sources, and providing education through newsletters, pamphlets, books, cassettes, and national conferences. The PSA also serves as a national reference source on the most current research and treatment methods in panic disorder and phobias.

The PSA can send you a national directory of therapists specializing in panic disorders and phobias. It can also, by telephone, provide you with the locations of treatment services nearest you. Hospital and university-based programs of comprehensive treatment will be listed in this directory, as well as other comprehensive centers including the TERRAP provider nearest you.

Be aware that not all providers listed in the PSA directory provide the most comprehensive or effective program of treatment. However, each listing will detail the particular orientation utilized as well as names, addresses, and telephone numbers to receive more detailed information. Remember to use the list of comprehensive treatment components we described in selecting the most thorough program in your area.

The national treatment directory as well as information on becoming a member of the PSA is available through:

>Phobia Society of America
>133 Rollins Avenue
>Suite 4B
>Rockville, Maryland 20852-4004
>Telephone: (301) 231-9350

2. The TERRAP Phobia Program

The TERRAP Phobia Program (an acronym for *ter*ritorial *ap*prehensiveness) is a nationwide, standardized program of treatment we highly recommend. This program is currently the only nationally available program for panic disorders and phobias that is professionally administered. This is especially important for panic victims who do not live near medical centers or hospitals offering comprehensive treatment. The TERRAP program offers *all* of the components we listed earlier in this chapter. Additionally, this program utilizes recovered TERRAP "graduates" as group assistants. These people serve as role models for group members just starting treatment. Their message, "I've been where you are, and I can help you recover too," is particularly helpful because the panic victim hears first-hand that recovery is possible.

TERRAP therapists are typically psychologists and are selected, trained, and supervised by the national and state directors of TERRAP, assuring quality control of treatment. They are usually independently based, with consulting psychiatrists for medication evaluation.

The founder of TERRAP, psychiatrist Arthur Hardy, has been directing this very successful program since

1971. He is currently on the board of directors of the Phobia Society of America and has served as president of that organization as well. We recommend that you contact the national office of TERRAP for locations of TERRAP providers nearest you as a primary step in selecting treatment sources:

> TERRAP Phobia Programs
> 648 Menlo Avenue #5
> Menlo Park, California 94025
> Telephone: (415) 327-1312
> (1-800) 2-PHOBIA

3. If Comprehensive Treatment Is Not Available in Your Area

You may find that comprehensive programs of treatment are too distant to serve as realistic treatment sources. In that case, consider one of the less comprehensive but closer programs listed in the PSA directory. Keep in mind that the most important components of treatment are those of desensitization or practice sessions, peer-group involvement, instruction in behavioral and cognitive techniques of anxiety management, and evaluation for medication.

The TERRAP Phobia Program has an excellent correspondence course for phobics and panic victims unable to reach a treatment group. This program consists of a comprehensive program manual detailing all relevant material for recovery, and tape recordings of TERRAP sessions to give the patient a sense of group inclusion. The recipient of the correspondence course is also able to have telephone contact (clarification, support, suggestions) with the staff of the TERRAP organization. Further information on the correspondence course and subscription information to the *TERRAP Times,* an informative newsletter for the professional and the recovering panic victim, is available by contacting the TERRAP organization in Menlo Park, California.

Again, regardless of the treatment source selected, we recommend that the panic victim seek more information about that specific source before entering treatment.

Step Four: Learn the Answers to Typical Questions about Comprehensive Treatment

The following questions are those most often asked by panic victims entering treatment or considering doing so. You may have heard similar questions from the panic victim or have been asked to answer these questions. We hope that the answers offered here will be useful to you and the panic victim with whom you interact.

1. The Thought of Entering a Group for Treatment Makes Me Even More Anxious! Why Is Group Treatment Stressed?

The group treatment format offered by most comprehensive programs is a tremendously helpful part of treatment. When panic victims meet one another, they realize that they are not alone, or crazy, as they often fear before meeting others who also panic, but are otherwise "normal" people. Group treatment provides each member with a strong support system, or "cheering section" in their work toward recovery. This is especially helpful for those victims whose general support system is weak, or those who hide their disorder from family and friends.

A group format also allows the panic victim to be both the *helpee* and the *helper* in treatment. While the members of a group have several commonalities in dysfunction, they also vary in individual areas of functional strength. Therefore, they are able to assist one another in group practice sessions conducted as part of treatment. For example, a young woman with a social phobia can easily help an agoraphobic woman enter a shopping mall. The agoraphobic woman can help that same social phobic by listening supportively to a short speech intended to build confidence in public speaking. This mutual support is extremely helpful in restoring self-esteem to panic victims who feel they are always in the dependent role with others. Such a program highlights a patient's strengths as well as areas of weakness. It also leads to strong friendships.

2. When Is the Best Time to Seek Help?

The sooner the better! Disorders of panic are treatable. Once you recognize the fact that panic and/or avoidance is beginning to affect your daily life (as well as the life of your family), it is time to seek comprehensive treatment.

It is important that a victim understand that, as a rule, panic disorders get progressively worse unless treated. As in dieting, it is easier to reach your goal if you have five pounds to lose rather than fifty. Panic victims who are aware of the urgency for treatment usually show the greatest motivation, and, consequently, the fullest recovery.

3. Won't I "Catch" Other Phobias or Fears from the People in My Treatment Group?

No! This is a phenomenon labeled "symptom swapping" by Dr. Hardy (1986). It is one of the very first questions addressed in a TERRAP meeting or other comprehensive treatment meeting. In a group session, you are there to concentrate on your *own* disorder and the various tools available to you to cope with your particular set of fears. You won't have time to "catch" other people's symptoms.

In many ways, comprehensive treatment groups are like classes, but the subjects you are studying are your panic and yourself. In fact, many programs require that you bring a notebook and that you take notes on group material. The focus is more on learning techniques and discussing how you are applying them than it is on group members describing their disorders.

When you *do* listen to other people in your program, it is actually beneficial to you. You realize that you are not the only one who experiences these feelings and has these physical responses. You learn skills that enable you to listen to others' problems *without* overempathizing with them, a common problem with phobia and panic victims. These skills enable you to listen and observe within the group and *outside* of the group without becoming overly emotional.

4. What If I Begin to Panic During a Meeting and Want to Leave?

No problem. No one understands this concern better than the other group members and your group therapist. Most comprehensive treatment programs have a standing agreement that members are free to leave, no questions asked. Usually, just knowing that you can leave if need be eliminates the sense of being trapped that leads to panic. Additionally, you will find that, because the other group members experience panic themselves, you are less afraid of becoming anxious in front of them. They will understand.

5. Wouldn't a Self-help Book Be Easier and Cheaper than Specialized Treatment?

Haven't you been dealing with your panic attacks and avoidance by yourself long enough? How successful have you been? Many panic victims have kept their disorder a secret from family and friends for years. They wouldn't dream of "imposing" their fears and needs on others. They often feel ashamed and alone in their disorder as well as disgusted with themselves for their inability to solve the problem. One of the first steps to recovery is recognizing the fact that you just can't handle the disorder on your own anymore.

Involvement in comprehensive treatment provides the panic victim with an expert professional directing you toward recovery. It also provides a peer group, people who have been through similar experiences. This supplies you with a cheering section, partners in the recovery process, and, in many cases, lifelong friends. While self-help books can be very useful, for a complete recovery, most panic victims require this comprehensive treatment and personalized professional guidance.

What about the expense? Phobics and panic victims usually focus their lives around others, placing their own needs last. It is time for you to realize that your needs are as important as theirs. Remember that while professional treatment does cost money, most insurance carriers pick up some or a majority of the expense. Additionally, most treatment centers will work with you to devise a payment schedule that is manageable for you.

Finally, while the initial outlay of money may seem costly at first, the return may well "pay off" for you in:

—salary and job advancement (now that you're no longer nervous about traveling, you can take that job offer in another town)
—less money spent on medication and medical treatment for your "nerves"
—your new ability to go on vacation and fun day trips
—access to old and new friends and social activities

—improved self-esteem and self-image
—getting your marriage and your life back to where you want them to be

6. Will I Ever Feel like a Normal Person Again?

With hard work and patience on your part, yes! Remember that panic disorder and phobias are treatable. But there is no magic cure. The road to recovery is one that involves practice and pitfalls along the way. Those who recover the fastest and most completely follow a comprehensive program of treatment conscientiously, and allow themselves the time to reach recovery.

Recovery will also be affected by other stress factors in your life. If you have a panic disorder and are working at a job you hate and come home to an abusive spouse, a high level of stress will prevail even though you have learned new skills to manage anxiety. In such cases, life-style and relationship changes will need to be made to maximize progress toward recovery.

A concluding thought: Things may be *better* than you expected with recovery. Often, people come into treatment with only one goal: not to feel so anxious! A comprehensive treatment program focuses not only on teaching the person to manage his anxiety better, but also to understand himself and others better. While you are learning how to fear panic less, you are also learning to like yourself more and to relate to others more successfully.

7. Since I Have Entered Comprehensive Treatment, I Am Having More Anxiety and Panic. Why?

This is a common phenomenon. You are now taking more risks. Instead of avoiding those situations and thoughts that formerly made you panic, you are now facing them, thinking them through, and confrontng them. Although your anxiety will increase as you tackle these situations and thoughts, you will be able to implement the skills you are learning to overcome these anxieties.

You may also have to deal with another aspect of these disorders, perhaps an unexpected one. As you start overcoming the panic attacks, and becoming less phobic, you may have to start dealing with other feelings and problems that were secondary to or even covered up by your anxiety. In some ways, having a panic attack may be more comfortable for you, less threatening than dealing with unsuspected feelings of unresolved grief, anger, or resentment in your life. The increase in anxiety you note may signal an urge to return to the "known evil" rather than the more frightening "unknown" of hidden thoughts and feelings. Be aware that, while most panic victims struggle with this dilemma, those who continue with treatment and work through their thoughts and feelings find a tremendous sense of relief and peace of mind. They state with certainty that this personal exploration is well worth any anxiety that accompanied it.

8. After I Recover, Will the Disorder Come Back Again?

No one's life is ever stress-free, and during periods of significant stress (e.g., the death of a loved one, pregnancy, separation) you may feel anxious. However, a comprehensive treatment program will teach you the tools to manage your anxiety and to prevent its progression to panic.

Remember that treatment is a process of recovery, not a cure. Like the dieter who has a binge day, panic may occur from time to time, but you will recognize potential triggers and successfully handle these stressful situations before they become overwhelming to you. In this way, you will develop a preventive, rather than a reactive life-style.

9. Can Medication Be Helpful?

Some people entering a comprehensive program do so with a long history of prescription drug use. Others enter with no such history and no real knowledge of the role that medication can play with these disorders. Medication can be a helpful component of comprehensive treatment in some cases. Some panic victims and phobics feel so disabled by their disorder that even getting through the day is an ordeal. They find that their ability to carry out needed everyday activities is so limited that they require the support that medication can offer, if only temporarily.

However, many phobics and panic victims experiencing significant distress and difficulty getting through the day are strongly opposed to even *considering* the use of medication. These individuals tend to be perfectionists, and perceive the use of any prescription drug as a sign of weakness on their part. Patients in a comprehensive treatment program are educated about the theoretical benefits of medication in panic and phobia disorders, and are given the option of meeting with an affiliated psychiatrist to evaluate if medication would be appropriate for them. The decision to pursue the use of medication deemed appropriate is always that of the panic victim. While many panic victims take advantage of medication as a help in initiating treatment and participating in practice sessions, they do so with the understanding that the medication will be decreased as their confidence and physical symptoms improve.

Specialists in this field recognize that many panic victims in comprehensive treatment who use medication attribute *any and all* improvement in functioning to the medication. This is of concern, since such individuals can develop a *psychological* dependence on the medication. Physical dependence or addiction to medication, specifically tranquilizers, is also a concern, and is closely monitored in treatment.

The ideal role of medication is in enabling the person experiencing severe anxiety to focus upon behavioral treatment (practice sessions) by reducing panic and anxiety symptoms. Therefore, the role of medication is presented as a temporary solution to panic when used in isolation, but, for some patients, a valuable part of comprehensive treatment leading to recovery. Many medication users are weaned from their medication by the end of a comprehensive treatment program, and many patients who used no medication at all recover as well or even better than those who did.

10. What Types of Medication Are Used for These Disorders?

First, it is important to understand that currently there is no medication that "cures" anxiety, panic, or phobias. While medication can be helpful in reducing some of the symptoms of panic disorder and disabling phobias, it is of greatest value when used in conjunction with a comprehensive treatment program.

Three types of medications are currently used to treat panic disorder, agoraphobia, and other anxiety disorders.

a. *Tranquilizers.* Tranquilizers are often prescribed to relieve the symptoms of anxiety and/or panic attacks. The action of the tranquilizer is limited; as the drug wears off, the anxiety will return. Tranquilizers are used on an as-needed basis, as well as on a scheduled basis. The most common side effect reported with tranquilizer use is that of drowsiness during initial use. Tranquilizers are physiologically addicting, and may result in psychological addiction as well.

b. *Tricyclic Antidepressants.* These drugs are taken daily on a regular basis. The dosage of the drug is carefully adjusted to receive maximum benefit. Symptomatic improvement is usually not evident for four to six weeks. The most common side effects reported with tricyclic antidepressants are dry mouth, blurred vision, and constipation. These drugs do not seem to be physiologically addicting, but may be psychologically addicting.

c. *Monoamine Oxidase (MAO) Inhibitors.* These drugs are also classified as antidepressants. The side effects, dietary restrictions, and constant medical monitoring associated with these drugs often outweigh the drugs' benefits. Side effects include dry mouth, blurred vision, constipation, as well as several others. Dietary restrictions must be strictly adhered to for the patient's safety. Prohibited items are beer, wine, aged meats and cheeses, and yogurt among others. Additionally, mixing these drugs with nonprescription antihistamines and decongestants can cause a blood pressure crisis, so the patient must be conscientious in adhering to instructions about the drug. While MAO inhibitors may be helpful to some patients, many report that they prefer to suffer the effects of their panic rather than worry about the side effects and possible dangers of their medication. MAO inhibitors do not appear to be physiologically addicting.

Many anxiety patients who have tried all of these medications have felt most positively about the tranquilizer used on an as-needed basis. It is common for panic patients to carry tranquilizers "just in case," without ever taking one. They report that just knowing they can take one if necessary results in a reassurance that is *naturally* tranquilizing.

11. What Can I Expect to Gain by Completing a Comprehensive Treatment Group?

Patients who conscientiously follow a comprehensive treatment program should expect the following gains by the end of a time-limited group (usually eight to sixteen weeks):

a. a moderate to significant degree of symptomatic relief
b. a moderate to significant improvement in behavioral functioning (reduced avoidance and escape)
c. a thorough understanding of their disorder and how to control it
d. insight into personal issues generating or maintaining anxiety that must be explored to enhance recovery
e. specific direction on how to proceed with more individualized treatment if needed
f. improved self-esteem
g. a peer support network

Many panic patients who needed professional help for stress much earlier in their lives only reached for help when the discomfort and inconvenience of their disorder outweighed their resistance to enter treatment. Consequently, many patients who complete a comprehensive program are suddenly able to attend to personal issues that were previously overshadowed or ignored because of the dramatic nature of their symptoms. A middle-aged woman can now deal with the unresolved grief of losing her mother in childhood. A young man can work to resolve guilt over being the driver in a fatal car accident. A young woman who is single and an only child can work through fears about her parents' failing health. A middle-aged, previously religious man can acknowledge and resolve feelings of anger with God about his wife's terminal illness. Both men and women can realize that their marriage is a source of stress and can be significantly improved with marriage counseling.

12. How Quickly Can I Expect to Recover?

Most experts in this field find that, generally, the sooner the panic disorder patient gets comprehensive, professional help for the disorder, the better the prognosis for early recovery. Of course, prognosis is also dependent upon the degree of other life stressors the patient experiences. For example, a young woman with a newly developed panic disorder who is married to an abusive spouse, has five children under the age of seven, and is undergoing eviction proceedings will probably not progress as far as a patient with similar symptoms who has a strong marriage, two manageable children, and financial security.

Strong motivation and the determined application of anxiety reduction techniques is also positively related to early recovery.

13. I'm a Wreck about What to Expect at the First Group Treatment Session. What Will It Be Like?

While various treatment programs may vary in the specific content of the first session, there is a common structure and atmosphere to most first session meetings. We will answer this question based upon the TERRAP program and our experience with typical first-meeting content and atmosphere.

First off, every group member arrives feeling like "a wreck"! Because most people have developed a full list of "what ifs" regarding the meeting, there is a rush for who will sit in the seat nearest the door. (What if I have to run out?) When this is acknowledged, in fact, everyone has a good laugh and begins to see the immediate bonding that occurs through common "what ifs."

The first session is one of the most enjoyable for the therapist to conduct. This is simply because we see such a tremendous transformation in each group member over the course of the two and a half hour meeting. They arrive feeling panicky, alone, and mentally kicking themselves for having had this "stupid" idea of a treatment group. They leave relaxed, talkative, and eager to return for the next session.

What could cause such a dramatic transformation? Simply meeting other "normal" people with a panic problem. In the TERRAP program, we spend time in that first session listing all of the "what ifs" the group members had imagined about the group and other group members. This is particularly fun because the group members are able to see humor in themselves and others as all of them admit that they expected to be the only "normal" one there. (Apparently they expected fangs and claws from others who suffer their disorder.)

By the end of the first TERRAP session, group members leave with a comprehensive overview of the treatment program, a realistic expectation of what they can expect with treatment and motivation, a new support group, a feeling of optimism about the future, and a loose-leaf notebook containing reading material and homework to be completed by the next session.

15. Why Do Books and Therapists Often Suggest Marriage or Family Counseling Once the Panic or Phobia Is under Control?

Often, with many of the phobics and panic victims we treat, dealing with the panic is only half of treating the disorder comprehensively. There are two reasons for this:

First, like an ecological system, when you make a change it effects the whole system. Both you and your spouse have had to make adjustments to the panic attacks or phobia. While your partner may be excited about your progress, he may also have mixed feelings about your new independence. Your improved ability to express youself may cause your husband to feel as if he is married to a stranger at times. These are problems that a couple will have difficulty solving unless they are able to work them out productively. Thus, your marriage may need treatment just like you did for your disorder.

A second reason for pursuing marriage or family counseling is that once your panic is under control, you will be able to focus on aspects of your family life that would benefit from change: a smoother-running household, scheduling more family fun time, and getting to know your spouse and children better now that your focus is more on things other than your physical sensations of anxiety. Without your panic, you may also be better able to hear the concerns of your family as well. Counseling can help clarify those issues and create a new spirit of comradery and optimism in your entire family.

16. How Does a Panic Victim "Measure" His or Her Anxiety?

It is mandatory for all panic victims to learn to measure their level of anxiety. It is also simple to do. It requires no machine, equipment, or tests. It simply requires that the anxiety victim understand a scale ranging from one to ten that represents ten different levels of anxiety from the mildest level (level one) to a full-fledged panic attack (ten). Comprehensive treatment programs instruct each participant in the use of this scale so that it becomes automatic for the anxiety patient to tune in to the body's level of anxiety and describe it with a number rather than with words.

Clinically, this scale is referred to as "SUDS" (*subjective units of discomfort scale*). It allows both anxiety victims and clinicians to work with *objective* terms during treatment, rather than wordy descriptions of anxiety symptoms that may vary from person to person. For example, one person might describe feeling "terribly anxious" while shopping. The clinician working with that person is confused. Does "terribly anxious" mean an anxiety attack or a level just below that? Or is it a more moderate kind of anxiety? "Oh no," the client might answer, "hellishly anxious is how I describe an anxiety attack!"

Progress is more readily determined and documented by using an anxiety scale. For example, a recovering agoraphobic can say that he or she can now shop at a grocery store at a two level of anxiety rather than an eight level. This represents a seventy-five percent improvement in functioning. This same person, using only words to describe that progress could say, "My shopping is significantly improved." But how could the clinician interpret that?

While not a science, phobia and anxiety treatment attempts to establish symptomatic measurement as objectively as possible to best design and monitor treatment. Use of the anxiety scale is just one of the methods used to accomplish this.

17. What Exactly Is the Systematic Desensitization Technique, and Why Is It So Important in the Agoraphobic's Recovery Process?

The systematic desensitization technique is a rather formidable sounding term for a very commonsense strategy. Basically, it is what its name infers—a gradual, step-by-step exposure of the phobic person to the type of situation he or she fears. And its importance in helping agoraphobics and other individuals who avoid certain situations or places for fear of feeling anxious cannot be over-emphasized.

Systematic desensitization is the technique used to teach children to swim, novices to drive, and musicians to play their instruments. In these cases however, there is usually little or no fear of the skill being mastered. It is simply the gradual approaching of a goal through very simple steps that are repeated until each of those steps in turn are mastered.

For example, the new driver is first taught about his vehicle. Next, he sits in the car in the driveway until he feels comfortable wth working all of the controls. Driving practices start out nice and slowly with an experienced and, hopefully, patient and encouraging driving instructor in the passenger seat. As simple driving is conquered on side streets close to home, more difficult driving is at-tempted as the driver ventures out with the support of his driving aide. Once the novice driver shows the compe-tence and confidence to venture out alone, the driving instructor keeps in close touch until that driver is deemed independent enough to drive longer and more difficult distances from home.

The drivers who progress fastest and most competently from novice driver to accomplished driver are those who are carefully guided through the rigors of the driving experience in a gradual, nonthreatening series of practices culminating in the skills required of a first-rate driver. Praise and encouragement are lavished upon that begin-ning driver by an experienced instructor who sets an ex-ample of ease and confidence behind the wheel.

Now let's explore the specifics of phobia treatment by giving a rather basic example of systematic desensitization. Suppose your happy-go-lucky ten-year-old was riding her bicycle down a street in your neighborhood. Let's also assume that, although your family does not own a dog, your daughter feels comfortable around dogs. Suddenly, a large dog she has never seen before rushes at the wheels of her bicycle, growling and pulling at her pants leg. Let's go on to imagine that this unfriendly dog managed to pull your daughter off of her bicycle, and to bite her in the leg, all the while continuing to growl and, basically terrifying your defenseless youngster. Happily, the dog's owner suddenly appears, perhaps equally as frightened by the incident, imagining your daughter's fear, and, perhaps, a large lawsuit as a result of this incident. This owner might be expected to be rather loud and threatening to the dog, thereby, in some ways adding fuel to your daughter's already well-developed trauma.

The episode might progress with the shaken owner and crying little girl locating you, her parent, listening to explanations of the incident from other excitable observers, and, finally a hurried trip to the pediatrician, most probably capped off with a preventive (and painful) shot of some nature. All in all, this would be a day that does not engender positive feelings for that particular dog, or perhaps, any dog your daughter might see following this incident.

Most parents would not be too surprised to observe a mild to moderate or even severe avoidance of dogs by this little girl. It might be shown as crossing to the other side of a street where dogs roam freely, or perhaps refusing to visit a dog-owning friend's house, or perhaps nightmares about dogs in general. At that point, an insightful parent would realize that this little girl had generalized her fear of the biting dog to all dogs. That same parent would realize that intervention would be necessary to prevent her from continuing to avoid situations or places where a dog might be present.

In this case, systematic desensitization would be an excellent technique to employ. Here, the goal would be to expose your daughter to dogs in a very gradual, non-threatening way so that she could relearn feeling comfortable in the presence of a dog. Following a well-thought-out talk with your daughter about a dog's fascination with moving things, and that some dogs are more excitable than others, and after commenting about how frightened she must have been, and what an unfortunate experience it was, your daughter would perhaps be as eager as you to resume feeling comfortable around dogs. However, this might be easier said than done because of her traumatic experience and the fact that she had been *sensitized* to dogs through this frightening experience.

A trained professional would develop a systematic de-sensitization *hierarchy* of exposure; basically a list of steps of exposure from the least difficult to the most difficult. That therapist might work with your daughter in mastering the following hierarchy:

Step 1: Look at cartoon pictures of puppies and dogs (Lady and the Tramp, various picture books of friendly looking dogs) until this step no longer generated any anxiety in your daughter.

Step 2: Look at photographs of friendly looking puppies and dogs until this step no longer generated any anxiety in your daughter.

Step 3: Stand outside of a pet store and look at the caged puppies for sale until this step no longer generated any anxiety in your daughter.

Step 4: Stand inside of a pet store and look at the caged puppies for sale until this step no longer generated any anxiety in your daughter.

Step 5: Pet a small, uncaged puppy in a pet store until this step no longer generated any anxiety in your daughter.

Step 6: Hold a small, uncaged puppy in a pet store until this step no longer generated any anxiety in your daughter.

Step 7: Pet a larger, uncaged puppy in a pet store until this step no longer generated any anxiety in your daughter.

Step 8: Hold a larger, uncaged puppy in a pet store until this step no longer generated any anxiety in your daughter.

Step 9: Walk down a street known to have a friendly, unleashed dog or two with your daughter until this step no longer generated anxiety in your daughter.

Step 10: Wait on the corner of that street while your daughter walked down the block alone until this step no longer generated anxiety in your daughter.

Step 11: Let your daughter walk down that street alone with you waiting at home for her return.

Reading through the preceding hierarchy is tedious, but provides a good overview of how such a plan is designed. Notice that for the most part, there is only one small change from one step to the next, thereby focusing upon only one new component to each step. Keep in mind that, while appearing rather simple, this technique is actually quite complicated to design most effectively. Designing and using the systematic desensitization hierarchy involves four very important aspects:

1. The phobic person must first be instructed in some basic relaxation techniques in order to learn to enter the practice situations in a more relaxed way, and to learn new ways of reducing anxiety generated by the practice hierarchy.
2. The input of the phobic person is extremely important in designing the hierarchy. No professional can design

a hierarchy without the help of the phobic who, after all, is the only one who knows which situation is more or less difficult to approach. It is also important to let phobics know that *they* are in control of each step. If any step on the hierarchy proves too anxiety provoking, they must feel free to leave that situation and regain their composure.
3. No step on the hierarchy should arouse the phobic's anxiety level to more than a three or four on the anxiety scale of ten. To do so could instill more fear in the phobic. Flooding, a technique whereby a phobic is exposed to the "worst fear" situation, or one evoking a ten on the anxiety scale, is *not* used in comprehensive phobia programs since this technique does not yield the more positive results of the very gradual systematic desensitization.
4. Praise and reward are extremely important in this procedure. The phobic must be praised for approaching their feared situations and rewarded for practicing. Regardless of how the practice session progressed, the professional will always find something praiseworthy in the phobic's performance.

Hierarchies developed for systematic desensitization with agoraphobics or other panic victims may involve a whole range of areas: learning to shop comfortably in a shopping mall, learning to shop at a grocery store without anxiety, driving distances from home, learning to eat in the company of others without anxiety, standing in lines without anxiety, learning to stay alone in the house without anxiety, crossing bridges without anxiety, socializing with others without anxiety, attending large gatherings such as sporting events without anxiety, etc.

Note that, while we use the phrase "without anxiety," this level of recovery comes only with dedicated practice of systematic desensitization hierarchies and the increase in confidence developed from experiencing many, many successful practices. Most of the phobics with whom we have worked have difficulty remembering experiencing anxiety in the situations for which they first entered treatment because they have conquered it so successfully.

18. I Panic Only at the Thought of Flying in an Airplane. Other than That, I Can Do Everything without Any Problem at All. Do I Need a Comprehensive Program to Conquer My Flying Phobia?

Many people investigate a comprehensive phobia program with the presenting complaint that they are unable to fly without panic. This often results in unhappiness on many fronts: the person who is unable or terrified to take a needed business trip, and the spouse and children whose husband, wife, or parent refuses any trip requiring flying. In interviewing such people, we often find that they experience anxiety in a number of situations, but that their avoidance of these other situations has been downplayed in comparison to the flying phobia. These individuals benefit from a comprehensive program where they learn specific skills to apply toward *all* anxiety-producing situations. Following completion of a comprehensive program, these people are able to generalize these skills to flying, driving, public speaking, and a whole series of situations that were mildly to moderately to significantly problematic before treatment.

For those people who have a clear-cut and specific fear of flying only, there are specialized programs that deal specifically with the fear of flying. Such programs are available in most geographical areas and are usually staffed by a professional therapist and a pilot of a large carrier plane. These programs are time-limited (usually four or so sessions), work with a group of flying phobics, and are comprised of instruction about typical plane flights, anxiety reduction techniques, and systematic desensitization to the flying experience.

Sessions are actually held at an airport, where the flying phobics meet with a uniformed pilot who explains the safety mechanisms of the plane, and has access to a grounded plane. Here, phobics can practice simply *sitting* on a plane without the pressure of an impending flight. A higher step on the desensitization hierarchy involves the pilot taxiing around the air field with the flying phobics, again without a takeoff. Finally, at the conclusion of the program, when all program members are feeling more confident, there is a "graduation" flight to a nearby destination.

These specialized programs can be highly effective. For the flying phobic desiring to work only on a fear of flying, such a program can be invaluable in helping them confront business trips and vacations they had previously avoided or endured with panic. To find a program near you, contact the Phobia Society of America for locations of specialized programs for fearful flyers:

Phobia Society of America
133 Rollins Avenue
Suite 4B
Rockville, Maryland 20852-4004
Telephone: (301) 231-9350

19. Why Are There So Few Men in Comprehensive Treatment Programs? Am I Likely to Be The Only Man in My Group?

It is true that many more women than men identify themselves as having an anxiety disorder. But tempting as it may be to assume that such disorders afflict females more than males, this may be an incorrect assumption. Many experts in the field of anxiety and phobia treatment believe that men may be just as victimized by anxiety disorders as are women. However, men appear not to report their difficulties as readily as do women for one or more reasons.

First, in our society, women are taught from infancy to be more attuned to their feelings and to express these feelings to others. Men, conversely, have gotten a message from infancy that it is somehow less "manly" to express vulnerability or feelings of fear. As a result, many men suffer with the same disorder as their female counterparts, but do so in silence. In fact, it is believed that many male victims of anxiety disorders are more likely to be found seeking relief from their anxiety *not* in a comprehensive treatment program, but through the use of alcohol as a "less-threatening" form of anxiety management. While societal training may work against the male by encouraging his silence about incapacitating anxiety, ironically, those same social structures may aid the male panic victim in confronting rather than avoiding his difficulty in functioning. While it is changing, many women are still able to remain at home if they choose to avoid an anxiety-producing situation: driving, shopping alone, social interactions, etc. The male in our society, however, is still largely forced into confronting that difficult drive to work each day, attending that crowded business meeting, driving across that bridge to earn that paycheck. As a result, many men are *prevented* from worsening their condition through avoidance of anxiety-ridden situations. And, although few recover completely without the aid of comprehensive treatment, their anxiety level is such that it enables them to maintain their daily functions, albeit with an uncomfortable level of anxiety.

Given that the male's activities are less often avoided than the females, and that men learn to keep feelings and perceived vulnerabilities to themselves, it is not surprising that more women than men seek out and enter comprehensive treatment programs.

Happily, this pattern is changing as more and more men become more comfortable with identifying themselves as anxiety victims in need of help. Consequently, there are increasing numbers of men in comprehensive treatment programs.

20. I Understand That Part of Comprehensive Treatment Is Teaching You How to Practice Difficult Situations with a Family Member or Friend as Well as a Professional Phobia Helper. How Do I Get Others to Help Me Practice?

First of all, you must choose the right practice partner. Not everyone can or should be a practice partner. Your support people need to respect this and realize that practicing with you is just one way to provide support in your recovery process. The husband you love but who tends to be critical or the neighbor who is a half hour late for every get-together are probably not the best practice partners you can choose. They may be sources of emotional support and encouragement, but not ideal for situations where you are following a rigorous program of systematic desensitization and anxiety management. Your practice partner must be someone you see as responsible and someone you can trust completely. It is a person with whom you feel comfortable talking about your anxiety and your need to take small steps on your terms. They must be dedicated and dependable so you can count on them being when and where they say they will be.

Once you have found this valuable person, just ask! Most often we have more difficulty asking for help than others do giving it. If you feel uncomfortable asking, you might set up a barter or exchange system where you baby-sit or bake that special cheesecake of yours, or put up storm windows in return for your partner's time. You can also ask that others give you practice time instead of gifts for birthdays and holidays. For example, your adult daughter might give you an hour of driving practice time on Wednesdays and Saturdays instead of a Christmas or birthday gift. A present of practice time is surely the gift that keeps on giving!

Step Five: Share Your Knowledge of Steps One through Four with Your Panic Victim, Mobilize Them to Comprehensive Treatment, and Continue Your Support from the Position of Informed Helper.

This final but difficult step is the most important: helping your panic victim to connect with the comprehensive road to recovery. Once this is accomplished, take the time to pat yourself on the back for the valuable role you have played. Chances are excellent that, because of your efforts, the life of the panic victim will show dramatic improvement.

3

How the Spouse (and Family and Friend) Can Help

Y ou've already begun. Just the fact that you're reading this book suggests that you have the four most important components for helping: the *time* to gather information, an *openness* to suggestion, *caring* enough about the panic victim to spend part of your life's time to help them improve theirs, and, hopefully, the *determination* to apply all that can be helpful. Feel good about this—you're a special person just for trying.

Some things to keep in mind while reading: First, while the word *spouse* is used when referring to the reader, most or all of these suggestions are helpful for the family and close support people of the panic victim as well. The terms *husband* and *wife* should also be considered interchangeable. Second, these points are relevant to the recovery process at different stages of the disorder: pretreatment, in treatment, and in recovery. While some may not relate directly to your phobic or panic victim, read them anyway. You may learn something that will be helpful.

Here is a list of the points you will understand more fully by the conclusion of this chapter:

1. Have a good, basic understanding of the disorder and the necessity for comprehensive treatment.
2. Be an advocate, not an enabler.

3. Help mobilize a spouse reluctant to seek comprehensive treatment.
4. Be your spouse's best friend.
5. Expect the road to recovery to be a long, rocky one.
6. Listen to the victims in comprehensive treatment. They're experts on their disorder and the steps to recovery.
7. Become a regular practice partner if asked.
8. Negotiate an "escape clause" with your spouse.
9. Show interest in the readings and other components of comprehensive treatment.
10. Praise, praise, and more praise!
11. Be prepared for and supportive of personal changes during treatment and recovery.
12. Be prepared for and supportive of social changes during treatment and recovery.
13. Keep a sense of humor!

1. Have A Good, Basic Understanding of the Disorder and the Necessity for Comprehensive Treatment.

If you have read the earlier chapters, you *should* have a good, basic understanding of panic and phobias and the need for comprehensive treatment. If you are still having difficulty understanding the dynamics of these disorders, you may be thinking: "But she used to be so normal!" or, "But why can't he do everything he used to do?" or "What's happened to the person I married?"

We find three examples helpful in making three important points. First, think of the actress Patricia Neal. For those of you unfamiliar with her or her personal history (beyond winning an Oscar for the movie *Hud*), she was stricken in her thirties with a massive stroke. At that time, she was at the height of her career. Defying predictions of permanent disability, Patricia Neal fought back, with the help and the "pushing" of her husband. As a result of professionally supervised retraining, tremendous effort, family support, and patience, Patricia Neal recovered, and went on to win an Academy Award nomination for her performance in *The Subject Was Roses*.

Point One:

A person, previously able to "conquer the world," may contract a massively debilitating disorder. But that same person, through comprehensive professional treatment, tremendous effort, family support, and patience, may recover, and, in many cases, lead a fuller life than that prior to the disorder.

It will be helpful for you to think of your spouse's disorder as you might think of a stroke. Although the stroke is a medical disorder and is therefore significantly different from disorders of panic, there are several similarities between these disorders: both may come on suddenly, seemingly without warning, and be mild, moderate, or devastating in their effect on the victim and the victim's family. While the disorders are different in origin, their effects are similar:

a. the primary victim (the stroke victim, phobic or panic sufferer) requires professional, comprehensive treatment to relearn skills that were previously simple
b. family members of the primary victim become secondary victims of the disorder according to the severity of the disorder
c. comprehensive treatment, combined with tremendous effort on the part of the victim, and the support of the family paves the quickest road to recovery

d. the victim must apply new skills and change old, bad habits to maintain wellness

e. the victim and the family can use the period of adversity to grow as individuals and to become closer as a family

As strange as it seems, panic victims who are unable to shop, be alone, drive distances, or do any number of things previously simple for them would almost welcome a disorder that would make their difficulty in functioning more understandable to those around them. They reason that victims of a severe injury don't face the pressure of explaining their change in functioning to family and friends.

A second example to consider is this: suppose your child, previously happy-go-lucky and independent, suddenly began avoiding school and began clinging to you, her parent. As this pattern continued, most responsible parents would seek professional help to explore reasons and remedies for the change in their child's behavior.

Point Two:

Do not deny adults the professional help and understanding they need *simply because they are adults.* Put the same degree of concern, action, and support into a change in your spouse's functioning as you would into your child's. Help your spouse find help, even if he or she is reluctant.

For the third example to help understand the disorder more fully, think of suffering a multiple leg fracture. If you yourself have experienced such a break, you know that, as with a massive stroke, basic skills must be relearned as your muscles, bones, and tissues heal. When you do reach full recovery, you may find, that even though your physician says you can resume playing tennis or running, that nevertheless there are times when the pain returns to your "fully healed" leg. This may be triggered by rainy weather, standing in long lines, dancing too many slow dances in a row, and sometimes for no clear reason at all.

For the panic victim in recovery, setbacks are shown in increased anxiety, and perhaps a panic attack or avoidance of situations that they had "conquered." Such setbacks may be triggered by times of increased stress, or a time of unhappy association, like the anniversary of a loved one's death. It may be Christmas or other holiday times when exposure to difficult family relationships is prolonged and disappointing in outcome. Asking a spouse about personal triggers for setbacks will be helpful to that victim by showing your concern, and helpful to you in illuminating reasons for changes in the victim's behavior and/or mood.

Point Three:

Even in recovery, the phobic or panic victim may experience a "setback." Expecting and understanding these episodes, and discussing them openly will help the victim return to his or her previous level of recovery.

2. Be an Advocate, not an Enabler.

Everyone needs an advocate at some time or another. If you have a legal problem, you need a lawyer to serve as advocate by explaining the options you have in solving your problem. An advocate is the friend who encourages you to go for that dream job you haven't quite got the courage to apply for alone. It's a colleague who gives you the pat on the back and an "atta boy" when you accomplish a difficult project. It's the person who gives you that little boost you need from time to time to help you be all that you can be. And, it's the person who is there to help you solve a problem when you feel there is no solution.

You, as a spouse, can be the advocate for your panic victim by doing preliminary legwork in exploring treatment sources and helpful books on panic or agoraphobia. An advocate is the person sitting down with the victim, *defining the problem,* and supporting the victim's efforts to improve:

> "Okay, you've got a disorder that's becoming more and more of a problem. This disorder has a name. It is treatable. Many people have had it, and, with hard work, have recovered from it. Let's deal with this situation in the most effective way. I'll help you get that help."

Just reading this book or a similar one about the disorder puts you in the role of an advocate . . . unless you are an enabler.

Enablers are rampant in the families of alcoholics:

a. the wife who phones her husband's boss and tells him that her husband (who is too drunk to stand) will be out with bronchitis
b. the parents who continually allow an intoxicated adolescent to return home at all hours of the night
c. the "understanding" husband who tells his adult children that he can't attend the granddaughter's dance recital because "Mom's having one of her days"

Enablers allow, in fact unwittingly *encourage,* self-defeating behavior to continue. The wife phoning her husband's boss prevents her husband from making his own phone calls and being responsible for his behavior. The parents who keep the door open until all hours for their adolescent drinker allow and even *encourage* that irresponsible behavior to continue. The grandfather who opts to stay with his intoxicated wife *allows* her behavior to control his day as well as hers (not to mention their children's and grandchildren's). As a result of their actions, enablers often delay or prevent the victim of alcoholism (and secondary victims—usually the family) from acknowledging their problem, confronting it, and working toward recovery.

No, this hasn't become a chapter on the evils of enabling the alcoholic. What it points out is that enabling goes on with many disorders. Enabling is usually done with the best of intentions, but with the worst of effects. Enabling the phobic and panic victim is no exception.

We'll spend a good amount of space on this point because it is so important and because it is often difficult to determine whether someone is advocating or enabling. Let's use another example to make it a bit clearer:

Let us imagine that your wife has suffered a skiing accident and has broken both of her legs. After the period of upset ("This is terrible!"–izing from family and friends) is over, adjustments have to be made. You, as the spouse, would *advocate* in the following ways:

—support your wife's emotional adjustment to loss of mobility
—take over the roles she has previously been filling (dressing and feeding the children, walking them to the bus, doing the laundry, shopping at the grocery store, etc.)
—contact a specialist to help her retrain muscles to strengthen her legs and improve her ability to walk
—support your wife's efforts in physical therapy sessions and in practicing what she has been assigned
—*then,* be willing to relinquish these roles as your wife recovers and becomes more and more able to resume her normal life.

As an *enabling* spouse, you would behave differently.
You would do the following:

—maximize the disability by allowing the "This is terrible!" discussion to go on ad nauseam
—take over the roles of dresser, feeder, shopper, etc., with no intention of ever relinquishing these jobs
—allow your wife to continue avoiding physical therapy sessions because she says she doesn't feel up to it each day
—continue to treat your wife as though she were victimized by a permanent, hopeless disease for which there is no hope or help.

With phobias and panic disorders, enabling spouses are the ones who continually perform roles for the victim; for example, driving, shopping, making excuses for declining party invitations. In other words, "helping" the victim *even though the victim refuses to get comprehensive help for the disorder.*

It's not fair. The enablers end up making all of the changes and compromises to keep life running as smoothly as possible. The victim, however, chooses the course of continued dysfunction over making a practical effort to improve. This doesn't mean that the victim is deliberately manipulative. What it *does* mean is that a failure to reach out to recovery forces the spouse and/or family to make all of the necessary adjustments to the disorder.

As an advocate, you can best help a spouse unwilling to pursue comprehensive treatment by making the disorder more of an inconvenience to your spouse. Don't always be available to "fill in" for your dysfunctional husband. Don't begin picking up all of the roles your wife is unable to fulfill. If you pick up all of the tasks your spouse can no longer perform, why *should* they seek to improve? Everything is getting done anyway!

Most of the phobics we have helped have come for treatment only after the *inconvenience* of their disorder outweighed their resistance to getting help. An agoraphobic young woman avoided help until her disorder was an obstacle to attending her best friend's wedding. A bridge-phobic simply avoided bridges for years until a job change required him to cross a bridge. Another woman whose agoraphobia prevented her from almost ever leaving her house and whose husband enabled her by doing nearly everything, entered treatment only when her husband's illness forced her to do more for herself. Ultimately, all of these people acknowledged the "push" that forced them to seek help and recovery. You can and should be that push for your spouse.

In short, the best role you can play as an advocate is this: assist your spouse's recovery by promising to help *as long as he or she promises to help too.* If your spouse is motivated in comprehensive treatment, you will be as helpful as that treatment recommends. While this may not be the most *popular* position you can take, it will be the most *helpful* in the long run.

Remember the movie *The Miracle Worker?* It traced the childhood of Helen Keller and the transition from a life of being enabled by her parents to a full, productive, and inspiring life. It was all brought about by the refusal of her teacher, Anne Sullivan, to enable Helen to be less than she could be. If you recall, Helen initially hated Ms. Sullivan for her advocacy. However, the full life that was opened to Helen through that advocacy finally convinced her that, in fact, Anne Sullivan was her greatest friend.

Remember this story when your stand of advocacy rather than enabling causes your spouse to accuse you of rejection or meanness or lack of love. Remember that enabling will not lead to recovery. Only advocacy—self-advocacy or the advocacy of others—will motivate the panic victim to seek help and to recover.

3. Help Mobilize a Spouse Reluctant to Seek Comprehensive Treatment.

One of the common difficulties of persons who develop a phobia or panic disorder is that they are nearly incapable of asking for help. This includes asking for understanding, favors, even the simplest of things that most people would be happy to provide. This difficulty often extends to an inability to ask for professional help for their disorders. Whether this mirrors low self-esteem, financial concerns, perfectionism, or something else doesn't really matter. What is important is that you must provide the mobilization for immobilized victims.

This can be a tricky role. You need information about comprehensive treatment sources, the steps to recovery, and also, you may feel, the negotiating powers of a Henry Kissinger. It's very hard when the victim refuses help—for whatever reason. It's hard on the victim, and it's hard on the family. In fact, in many ways, it is similar to the alcoholic who, by refusing to acknowledge and treat the alcoholism, subjects the entire family to the serious ramifications of the disease.

The good news is that most phobics and panic victims are eager to get help. Those who aren't usually can be persuaded by their spouse if that spouse promises their moral support, and offers to do the preliminary legwork in connecting with a comprehensive treatment source.

This is where you are so necessary: you can locate the treatment source, offer to accompany your spouse to the consultation session and obtain starter books about the disorder for your spouse. (The books by Claire Weekes mentioned in the bibliography are highly recommended.) Sometimes providing an option (treatment) with some "think time" for them to mull things over allows the victim to make the decision to mobilize. Think of it as planting a seed for thought and action.

For those of you having extreme difficulty encouraging your spouse to take action for treatment, consider taking the following steps: First, become familiar with the disorder by reading this book carefully. Second, obtain one of the Claire Weekes books on the subject: *Hope and Help for Your Nerves*. This paperback speaks directly and reassuringly to phobia or panic victims. It shows them that they are *not crazy,* that they are *not* having a nervous breakdown, that they are *not* alone, and that they are *not* a hopeless case. Many previously reluctant victims have been persuaded to seek professional help after reading Dr. Weekes's reassuring words. You might be the one to offer the book to your spouse telling him or her that this is known to be a very helpful work and contains information to reach recovery.

Next, refer to chapter 2 of this book, to determine how to locate a comprehensive treatment source in your area. Phone the source, explain your spouse's condition, and ask for further information about treatment. Finally, tell your spouse all that you have learned about the treatment source, assure them of your full assistance in exploring treatment, and ask if they would be willing to attend a consultation session with you there for moral support. Most specialists are very understanding of the victim's fear of reaching out for help and are happy to set up an introductory or exploratory session to help allay those fears. Such a session usually puts the panic sufferer more at ease. The "unknowns" that lead to anxiety-provoking "what ifs" regarding what the therapist is like, and what the treatment is like become "knowns," and less a source of anxiety.

If your spouse is agreeable, have him or her call for a consultation session. Most victims will agree to this since they will have some control over the situation. (If your spouse asks *you* to call, allow yourself this one act of enabling if it means that he or she will follow through.) Should your spouse refuse, table the discussion temporarily but state that you will want to discuss it again in a week. Then do so.

There is, of course, a very delicate balance between *supporting* victims making the decision to get help and *pushing* them. Use your best judgment. Usually patience pays off, especially when the victims realize that others are being "disabled" by their disorder as well. The panic victim or phobic agrees to take at least a small step toward committing to treatment. Whether it's reading a Claire Weekes book, or phoning a specialist, that all-important first step *will* be taken.

4. Be Your Spouse's Best Friend.

This simple but difficult directive will make all the other suggestions much easier to follow. Research tells us that the key to the marriages that succeed in quality and longevity is that each partner considers the other a very best friend. This means that they confide in each other, and confide nothing to others of which their spouse is unaware. When you are your spouse's best friend, you leave the door open for that overused, misunderstood concept of communication. Basically, it simply means this: treating your spouse the way you would like to be treated, and talking and listening to your spouse the way you would like to be talked and listened to. That's right—the Golden Rule.

Transactional Analysis therapy (Harris, 1973) explains it as having adult-to-adult conversations. This means no criticizing, no "I-know-better and you're-a-nitwit" tone. It also means not overdoing it with sympathy and help, à la "You're just a little boy in a grown-up body, but don't you worry, I'll take good care of you and fight all your dragons for you" comments.

By establishing this best-friend relationship with your spouse, you establish the kind of relationship and create the kind of environment in which they can tell you what they're feeling, what they need, how you can best help them, and, eventually, what will be most likely to get the entire family "back to normal." Needless to say, this means being the exact opposite of the following gruesome four: (a) punitive, (b) judgmental, (c) inapproachable, and (d) sarcastic.

It isn't surprising that among married victims of panic, those who recover most satisfactorily have successful marriages and strong support from their spouses.

5. Expect the Road to Recovery to Be a Long, Rocky One.

Perhaps the biggest mistake a spouse or other support person can make is to expect progress to be continuous. For example, it is common that a phobic in treatment can suddenly enter a shopping mall after months or even years of being unable to do so. Everyone, including the victim feels euphoric! But then something else happens. The spouse, or other family members, in great enthusiasm, begins making plans: a European vacation, a standing-room-only theater engagement, a shopping trip to a popular new mall during Saturday's busiest time. The victim feels a sudden new sense of panic: the panic of feeling "locked in" to performing well (phobically) or disappointing everyone close.

Some guide words to help with this problem: *patience, patience, patience.* Just as you weren't ready to tackle the Los Angeles freeway after your second driving lesson, so the panic victim isn't ready to take leaps and bounds immediately after the first success or two. Expect progress to vary: a good day on Tuesday, a not so good Wednesday. Be patient; it's all part of recovery.

6. Listen to the Victims in Comprehensive Treatment. They're Experts on Their Disorder and the Steps to Recovery.

For those of you with spouses, family members, or close friends in comprehensive treatment, feel assured that they are receiving valuable instruction on how best to recover. Don't underestimate their knowledge of how you can best help them. *Ask!* In all family support sessions we have held, the question most often asked is (you guessed it), *"How can I help my spouse?"* The best answer is, *"Ask them!"* We can supply general suggestions but the most valuable and specific way you can help your spouse is to ask, "How can I best help you?" and then *listen* to the response. And, don't just ask once. Ask each time you're feeling frustrated in not knowing how to work with him or her. Ask again! A victim may want to be distracted on Monday during a surge of panic, but reassured on Friday when anxious. On Saturday he or she may want to get away from the situation altogether, and on Sunday, be energized to ride it out. Probably the first item on every panic victim's "wish list" is the simple desire to be listened to, *really* listened to, by family and friends.

We surveyed the phobics and panic victims who have completed or are currently completing the TERRAP program we offer, and asked, among other things, "How could your *spouse* best help you in dealing with your disorder?" Here are the comments they offered that were most representative:

"First, accept the fact that I have a problem that doesn't make me any less of a person because of it. Be more understanding and talk with me about my phobia more often. Be more understanding. Learn about my phobia through me or through literature and try to help me through practices or by talking."

"By not forcing me into a situation; by understanding and communicating with me about my phobia more often."

"Just be more attentive, eager to assist with my practices. Listen more."

"Talk to me. Try to reason with me. Hug me. My husband never got angry or impatient with me."

"Talk to me more, and listen to what I have to say. Let me plan an activity from start to finish to let me feel more normal. Hold my hand and show affection for no real reason. When my husband let me know he cared and that I didn't have to perform, it was a big boost for me."

"Listening to my feelings no matter how unimportant they seem to him and just 'validating' them instead of saying, 'Just think positively!' or 'That's ridiculous!'"

"By your support, acceptance, practice support regularly, understanding, willingness to find ways to help."

"Listen and try to understand that no matter how tired you are, it will be worth it."

"Don't overreact. Give me a hug and reassurance."

"Recognizing that the improvement I make is a *big deal* and talking to me about it."

When we asked those same people, "How could a *friend* best help you in dealing with your disorder?" the answers were generally similar, but with some interesting variations. Here are representative comments:

"My friends could be more helpful by pushing me more since I'm bad at asking for help. I think they think that this means that I don't need help. What it really means is that it's hard for me to ask for a favor."

"By saying, 'That must be difficult,' instead of saying something like, 'I can't imagine that someone like you would have a problem.'"

"By understanding that if I'm not comfortable and I want to leave, we can leave and not make a big deal over it."

"Stay calm when I'm having an anxiety attack. Try to distract me."

"A friend could be especially helpful by letting me know that, if our relationship becomes less close, that it was not due to my phobia."

* * *

As you can see, while a common feature of individuals who develop such disorders is a tendency to hold in thoughts and feelings, *when asked,* they have a lot to say about how they would like to be treated. Can you see the commonalities in the preceding comments? What the panic victim requests is: "Talk to me, listen to me, learn about me, respect me, practice with me, touch me, and be my partner in reaching recovery."

In our clinical experience, those panic victims who have recovered most fully and most quickly were highly motivated people with spouses, family, and friends who recognized and fulfilled each of their panic victim's needs. That husband or wife's reward was a stronger marriage and a greater ability to enjoy that marriage in a variety of settings and situations. For the family and friend of the victim, the reward was a stronger relationship, and a person able to reciprocate in offering support.

As the spouse, family, or friend of a panic victim, learn of your own victim's special needs. Ask.

7. Become a Regular Practice Partner If Asked.

For those of you with a phobic spouse in specialized treatment, you will learn through your spouse and his or her therapist how best to carry out "practice sessions." These usually involve accompanying your spouse into the situations that are so difficult for them in a very gradual, step-by-step manner. This may mean following your driving-phobic by one car length around the block over and over again. It may mean separating from your mall-phobic for only two- or three-minute intervals at a time. Or perhaps you will be required to frequent fast-food places to order a take-out soda to help your phobic recover from a fear of crowded places. These practice sessions are the foundation of recovery.

One of the best gifts you can give your spouse, better

than a pearl necklace, better than a compact disk player, better than a designer watch, is the gift of your time for practice sessions. One of our TERRAP members received a small, beautifully wrapped box from her grown daughter at Christmas. Inside was a gift certificate entitling the recipient to practice driving sessions every Saturday morning until the recipient deemed it no longer necessary. It would have been difficult to find a happier mother that day. That ongoing, most thoughtful of gifts is credited with the speed of that phobic's recovery. In fact, this recovered agoraphobic (once housebound) now serves as a group assistant in our program.

It is important to note that some phobics will prefer a practice partner other than you. Respect their choice. It doesn't mean that they care less about you, it simply means that they feel they will recover more quickly with a different partnership for these sessions. You can be supportive in a number of ways. Acting as a practice partner is just one of them. Ask about another that would be helpful.

8. Negotiate an "Escape Clause" with Your Spouse.

Panic victims are more likely to attempt anxiety-provoking situations if they know that they can leave if they need to. Most phobics and panic victims avoid situations involving crowds or structured social events (movies, parties, dining out, sporting events) for fear of creating a fuss if they feel the need to escape. This fear of disappointing or angering or worrying a spouse, family, or friends creates additional anxiety for the victim. You can help by making a contract with them:

"You (the victim) give it (the party, movie, restaurant, wedding) a try, and I (the spouse) agree to leave with you immediately (or stay while you leave, if you prefer) when you give me the prearranged signal (a squeeze of the hand, etc.)."

Many of our recovered phobics have found that this kind of arrangement took tremendous pressure off of them. In turn, they were much more likely to tackle situations they had previously avoided. Most said that just *knowing* that they could escape if they needed to made it less likely that they *felt* the need to escape. The result: the victim *and* the spouse were happier.

9. Show Interest in the Readings and Other Components of Comprehensive Treatment.

Many comprehensive treatment programs provide their patients with reading materials and suggested readings. The TERRAP program, for example, provides participants with a nearly four-hundred-page treatment manual written by Dr. Hardy to guide the panic victim through the course of treatment. Your spouse will be tremendously grateful for any interest you show in these materials. First, because it indicates an interest in something that is so important to her, and, second, because these materials can be extremely helpful to you in better understanding the disorder and the road to recovery. Ask your spouse how the treatment session went. While specific information about other group members is confidential, your spouse can tell you what the group is learning, how the group process is evolving, and his or her thoughts and feelings as each week of treatment passes. Our experience has been that, following treatment, many recovered group members stay in touch, and, often the spouses have a lot in common as well. In fact, one strong friendship started between two husbands of panic victims who met in the waiting room of our offices. Today, these two couples, the recovered wives, and the husbands with so many experiences in common, are the best of friends.

Again, sharing the recovery experience with your spouse will result in the best recovery, and a strong feeling of inclusion on your part in this very exciting transformation.

10. Praise, Praise, and More Praise!

Every victim of panic knows discouragement and self-doubt. Since it is such a rocky road to recovery, it's human to feel discouraged and that the "light at the end of the tunnel" has been extinguished! That's where you come in. Remind your spouse of how far they've come when they see no progress. List with them the things they are now able to do that were nearly impossible a short time ago. Tell them how much you admire their perseverance and their commitment to improve. And, finally, remind them that it is okay to feel discouraged at times.

This same need for praise is necessary for happy times as well. It may seem absurd to you that your spouse is boasting about entering the local grocery store's vegetable department "with only a three-level of anxiety!" In fact, you may not even know what a "three-level of anxiety" is! But, remember Patricia Neal. Your spouse needs your praise and shared excitement with each small step toward recovery as if he or she were taking a first step after suffering a massive stroke. It's the same kind of progress.

11. Be Prepared for and Supportive of Personal Changes During Treatment and Recovery.

One of the most confusing, worrisome, and yet exciting parts of treatment for phobics and panic victims is the change they recognize in how they feel about things, and how they react to things. Many report that they have never felt so terrible and so wonderful at the same time. It's as though they go through the struggle of giving birth to themselves, simultaneously encompassing the pain and worry of a difficult labor as well as the euphoria and pride that comes with the birth of a beautiful, healthy new life.

It is important to remember that one of the biggest fears of people most likely to develop phobias and panic is the fear of losing control and looking foolish. Related to that fear is the almost overpowering desire of these people to be nearly (in fact, completely!) perfect. By appearing perfect, they feel that they will be liked by everyone, and, therefore, never be abandoned. With this in mind, you can understand how a comprehensive treatment program stressing independence and assertiveness would have a dramatic effect on the panic victim.

Treatment encourages panic victims to express feelings of loss, joy, and a myriad of other emotions both positive and negative in a verbal or active way. They learn *not* to express their feelings through body symptoms such as shortness of breath, palpitations, sweaty hands, feelings of weakness, tension headaches, and so on. As a result, often for the first time, persons in treatment experience what they feel *directly*, instead of converting it into a physical symptom. The relief felt as a result is often monumental.

The personal changes resulting from comprehensive treatment can be quite marvelous. A woman who was unable to swallow without anxiety about choking realized that she had been holding back all kinds of things that she needed to say. It was as if she got as far as knowing what she wanted to say, but choked back her words from the fear of saying it all wrong and losing control of her anger. She learned that her greatest worry in expressing herself was that she would anger or hurt those she cared about, resulting in rejection and abandonment.

Do you see in this woman's fears the two issues we identified as basic? First, the fear of losing control, and secondly, the fear of abandonment. If you listen carefully to what your own panic victim is saying you may identify similar issues.

In many ways, treatment and recovery results in the patient going through something very similar to what most of us go through in adolescence. It's called *individuation*. It sounds more complicated than it is. Individuation is really just the realization that one is a person all by oneself, with one's own special values, preferences, goals, and talents. With successful individuation one *allows* oneself to act on those preferences and goals, even if it means disappointing a parent (choosing the college that *I* want instead of the one my parents prefer).

Individuation develops that part of us that allows us to get out of a no-win situation without feeling guilty about it. For example, you can move out of your parents' home when the generation gap finally results in everyone being unhappy with everyone else's behavior. You are able to live your life the way you wish, even when your parents want you to live your life the way *they* want you to live it. It follows, then, that in successful individuation, you are able to accept that others view you as less than perfect (your parents, for example). In fact, it is also okay for you to view *them* or others as less than perfect.

Your spouse will be undergoing a kind of individuation as he or she recovers from the disorder. As a result, he or she may totally baffle you with the "personality changes" made during treatment. One day your spouse may be teary, the next day on top of the world. Or your spouse may return from a group session vowing never to return, and, the following day comment on how much he or she is looking forward to the next meeting.

The point is that your spouse will *not* be learning to be a different person than he or she was before treatment. Rather, your wife or husband will be learning to develop fully as a person by discovering "who they are," faults and all. As a result, your panic-plagued husband will learn that it's okay to express feelings—even for a man! He will learn that he won't turn into a monster if he expresses anger, just as he won't cry a river of tears when he expresses his love.

Recovering phobics and panic victims learn that it is okay to cry, happy tears or sad, even if you're a man. They learn that it is okay to be imperfect. They learn that contrary to what they might have believed, most people prefer people who are not perfect. Our faults and vulnerabilities make us more interesting and less intimidating to all the other imperfect people out there.

What will these changes mean to your marriage? In a word, change. One partner can't change without the other partner changing. It is a matter of two people adjusting to each other. When the spouse is supportive, the change can be wonderful—for the primary victim, for the spouse and for the entire family. So, when you see your wife becoming more open about how she feels, be glad. Now you know where she stands. When you see your husband making new choices for himself, like changing his job or having less contact with an irritating relative, respect that he is making changes that he feels are necessary for him to be the best that he can be.

All in all, you will find that your spouse will be relating to you more as an adult to an adult, no longer as a helpless child to a nurturing or critical parent. Your openness to this new model of your spouse, and your willingness to discuss what he or she has learned about himself, how he or she operates as an individual, and how he or she wants to change can open the door to a better marriage than ever before.

12. Be Prepared for and Supportive of Social Changes during Treatment and Recovery.

Just as panic victims make changes in the way they think and feel, so they make changes in the way they operate as a social being. This sounds very clinical, and as if we're studying a bug under a microscope, but basically, it boils down to this: When engaged in a comprehensive treatment program, your spouse will be meeting with other victims of phobias and panic. For most people, this is the most enjoyable, enlightening, and helpful aspect of treatment. Suddenly they realize that they really *are not alone*, just as all the self-help books have said. They meet people with the same fears and frustrations and confusion and questions. They feel accepted and understood. And they often make deep friendships that continue long after treatment has ended.

How will this impact on you and your marriage? Very strongly. And that impact may be both positive and negative, depending upon the quality of your marriage before treatment and your acceptance of your spouse's new outlook during treatment. For example, the wife that was so totally dependent upon you, and so effusive in her praise of your patience and support may become far less dependent upon you. While this may sound positive (and indeed it is), it may also seem as if a very special part of your relationship is gone: that bond that you shared when only the two of you were fighting this thing together.

You may find that, while before, *yours* was the only voice that could calm your husband during a surge of anxiety, now there are several other supporters, people in his group who can help him. They can help because they are peers. They understand in a way you never can because they experience what he experiences. It makes sense, of course, but you may still be surprised to see a little of the green-eyed monster, jealousy, creep into you.

You may find yourself becoming irritated at the large number of phone conversations that your wife has as part of the treatment. The telephone is always busy when you need it. (Or is it simply that she seems to enjoy talking with that other panic victim so much?)

All of this may be especially confusing to you because you may remember thinking that you would give anything if only your wife were not so dependent upon you and was able to make gains toward recovery. And now, that previously shy, often withdrawn woman you were so worried about seems to be going through a kind of adolescent telephoning addiction and spending more time out of the house and away from you than ever before. In fact, she seems pretty happy about it and doesn't even notice that you, the one who was always there when no one else was, has been "left behind" in the wave of her new life in recovery. In fact, you may find yourself yearning for life the way it was *before* she got treatment and began to improve so dramatically.

How do you deal with these very human, certainly understandable, but a little embarrassing thoughts and feelings? First of all, acknowledge them to yourself. Next, allow yourself the luxury of understanding how you could feel this way. It might be helpful to think of a nonrelated, but similar kind of situation to put your feelings into perspective. For those of you who are parents, remember what it was like waiting for that first pregnancy to blossom and deliver? If you are a woman, you probably found yourself instinctively feeling very close to perfect strangers who were obviously in the same pregnant condition you were in. If you are a man, you might have been eager to ask another first-time father how *he* was dealing with the excitement, worry, financial concerns, and, after delivery, the sleepless nights of late feedings.

Suddenly, you might have found your interest in old friends who were *not* first-time parents waning, and your interest in newer friends with infants of a similar age growing. If you're like most parents, you might have been horrified to find yourself, male or female, debating the relative merits of Pampers versus Huggies diapers when running into other new parents at a party.

The point is that no matter what the situation, if it is a new one for us, we have a tremendous need to "compare notes" (thoughts, reactions, feelings, experiences) with others encountering the same situation for the first time. This is what is happening with your wife and the other members of her treatment group. You may feel that you have been replaced, forgotten, rejected, or passed over for others, but don't be discouraged.

Take the time to let your spouse know how you are feeling. This will require tact, and it will also require cutting through to the real issues: (*a*) you are feeling left out, (*b*) you are concerned that her recovery may distance you, and (*c*) you miss your special time together.

Very few people become defensive when being told that they are loved and missed, and that is basically what you will be saying to your spouse. Work out with your partner how this situation can be remedied. While recognizing that she needs to keep in touch with others in treatment with her and that she must become more independent of you, explain that you need to be included in the recovery process in some way as well. Such a conversation and request may result in a new closeness for you during the recovery process.

And remember, just as we return to old friends once the novelty of new parenthood wears thin and the discussions about diapers become boring, so will your recovering spouse remember you. And the best part is that it will be an even better spouse.

Keep in mind that the effect of your spouse's treatment on your marriage will depend heavily upon the quality of your marriage prior to treatment. If your relationship was not as close and supportive as it might have been before treatment, your spouse may utilize new relationships to compensate for the weaknesses in your marriage. If this is so, you might consider some focused marriage counseling sessions to learn to redefine and strengthen your marriage. Suggest it!

In most cases, although the person in treatment forms close bonds with others in treatment, the bond with a previously loving and supportive spouse grows even stronger. The tension that was there from needing to make life-style adjustments to the disorder dissipates and the new experiences the couple can now share restore or create a deeper level of togetherness.

13. Keep a Sense of Humor!

Where would we be without a sense of humor? Humor can get us through the toughest times. In fact, sometimes it's *only* our sense of humor that gets us through those times. Humor is our ability to laugh at the absurdity of life's hassles and at our own special foibles. It's what has made Erma Bombeck a wealthy woman and what keeps her readers reading her columns and books. Humor allows us to take a lighter perspective of stressful events, pain, the unfairness of life, and of our own inability to be perfect.

Multiple studies have shown the very positive effects of optimism, humor, and laughter on coping with stress and even life-threatening disease. Norman Cousins, author of *Anatomy of an Illness as Perceived by the Patient* (1979), tells of his own experience with a life-threatening illness. Bedridden, he refused to "give in" to the disease. Instead, he spent hours watching episodes of *Candid Camera* and Marx Brothers films in an attempt to "laugh away" the disease process. Not only did he recover from that illness, but his success with this unorthodox method of self-help resulted in university-based research on the stress and disease reduction properties of humor and positive thinking.

Of course, there are plenty of people who don't seem to have a sense of humor. We all know some. They are the people we're likely to see swallowing multiple aspirins for tension headaches, leaning on their car horns for the least little traffic infraction, and taking themselves, others, and the world entirely too seriously. What is the point? Just this. As the spouse of someone with an anxiety disorder, you have a choice. You can view it as something terrible, maddening, unfair, and the worst thing that could possibly happen to you and your spouse. Or, instead, you can view this disorder as an inconvenience; something that you wish you had more control over, but which has to be dealt with step by step.

You can also look for the lighter side of the disorder. It is our experience that the patients with whom we've worked who had the best senses of humor have progressed the furthest. How is this possible? Simple. If we tell ourselves that something is terrible, our system will react as if it *is* terrible. Our physiological defense systems will be called into play to "protect" us from the evils we anticipate. However, if we tend to look at the lighter side of dealing with such disorders (and there are always several lighter sides!), we not only reduce the stress we feel, but actually make it more likely that we master the steps to recovery.

Let's get specific by acknowledging some rather funny situations that can arise in the treatment of these disorders. One very elderly woman with whom we worked needed to practice on her phobia of elevators. When she had progressed to practicing by herself, her worry, she reported to the group, was whether or not the elderly elevator operator viewed her multiple trips each day as real business or a veiled attempt to establish a romantic relationship with him.

The husband of one of our store phobics noted that he had learned to really hate bananas. It seemed that his wife was practicing entering a grocery store over and over again, purchasing something as quickly as possible near the front of the store. Bananas were right at the front in the fruit department. Several trips later, and after days of banana splits, banana bread, banana milk shakes, and creamed bananas on toast, her husband asked seriously if it was possible for her to change the practice store or at least the fruit she bought. He requested apples.

One of the goals of a comprehensive treatment program is to teach the victim of panic, and the family as well, to keep the disorder in perspective. Many patients enter a program with a history of treating their disorder very, very seriously—so seriously that they have given it tremendous power over their lives. It is almost as if the disorder has a life of its own. Only by moderating this potentially destructive force through humor can you keep it from generating feelings of self-blame, anger, and hopelessness.

4

How the Therapist (or Counselor) Can Help

The therapist or counselor of panic victims is in a key position to help that victim. Often, by the time these patients reach you, they have already consulted with a physician and by contacting you, are demonstrating a desire to pursue their disorder through a therapeutic approach. Conversely, the panic victim may contact you as a first step to finding answers about what is happening to them. This chapter will prepare you to pave the road to recovery for each of these individuals.

This chapter is predicated upon the following understandings:

1. Patients presenting to a therapist with a panic disorder, agoraphobia, or a disabling simple phobia want specialized help providing symptomatic relief and improved functioning as quickly as possible:
   (a) a truck driver experiencing panic on the road fears for his job if the panic cannot be controlled
   (b) a mother of three yearns to shop with her children, attend open school nights, and take family vacations like she used to
   (c) an executive terrified of elevators faces panic each day following his transfer to a skyscraper

    (d) an elderly woman requiring surgery postpones it
        for fear of losing control in the hospital
2. Symptomatic relief and an improvement in the performance of daily activities is the first priority of the patient and the therapist in treatment planning
3. There is a recommended program of comprehensive treatment for panic disorder, agoraphobia, social and disabling simple phobias
4. Specific issues that are relevant to the development and maintenance of the anxiety disorder are of importance in treatment planning *following* symptomatic relief and improvement in functioning
5. A comprehensive treatment program and more traditional issues-oriented therapy compliment one another. A program reducing anxiety enables the patient's focus to shift from bodily symptoms to core issues of relevance
6. The role of any competent, ethical therapist is to provide the most effective treatment for the patient or to refer that patient to such a treatment source

Our strong opinion in this matter is based upon the literature on recommended treatment for panic disorder and agoraphobia and other phobias, as well as our work with such victims and their comments about earlier attempts to get help. In most cases, patients came to us after years of trying to conquer their panic attacks and agoraphobia. While they had had years of therapy, they saw no significant improvement in their ability to control their anxiety.

They reported having had a wide range of treatment strategies: psychoanalysis, support therapy, biofeedback, hypnosis, marriage counseling, and others. Some had components of the comprehensive program of treatment, but the effect of this partial program was basically ineffective in improving their ability to function without panic. Each time they had entered therapy believing that they would be treated with the best-known methods for their disorder. And each time, after several months of therapy, they came away feeling that they were not being helped the way they needed to be helped. And so they moved on to a new therapist with the same hope that this next time would be different. But the basic result of the therapy was the same. They were still unable to perform daily activities without panic. And now they had new problems to contend with:

(a) The truck driver, continuing to panic on the road, had left his job on disability. This resulted in financial stress, marital stress, family stress, low self-esteem, and depression.

(b) The mother of three continued to avoid family activities requiring her to confront her anxiety. This resulted in marital stress, family stress, low self-esteem, and depression.

(c) The executive, an elevator phobic, changed jobs to avoid having to use an elevator. This resulted in loss of job seniority, financial stress, marital stress, family stress, loss of previous working friendships, low self-esteem, and depression.

(d) The elderly woman postponing surgery underwent emergency surgery, resulting in trauma, increased anxiety regarding hospitals, and a stronger determination to postpone exploratory surgery on a breast tumor. This resulted in a health risk, marital stress, family stress, low self-esteem, and depression.

As a therapist coming in contact with such patients, here is how you can prevent these disorders from evolving to such complicated dimensions:

1. Recognize the All-important Role You Play in Diagnosing the Disorder and Paving the Road to Comprehensive Treatment.

As a therapist seeing a patient for the first time, the role you play may be the most important one of all: putting the patient in touch with the best source of comprehensive treatment for recovery. Ask any recovering member of a comprehensive treatment program what the biggest frustration of all is, and most will tell you this: the time they feel they lost by not being referred for comprehensive treatment of their disorder when they first presented their symptoms to a medical or mental health professional. They relate histories of therapy that were helpful in developing insight into how they operate as an individual; why they think and feel the way they do. But they feel angry, and in some cases, betrayed, that they were not routed to the most effective program of treatment that was available to them to learn to control their panic and improve their everyday functioning. Here are typical comments from patients completing the TERRAP program after several previous attempts to get help:

"I needed my therapist to tell me what I had. I went to several before I was properly diagnosed and told where to go for specialized help."

"My therapist never zeroed in on the panic disorder, so we never really discussed the techniques and issues that I later learned were so important to talk about."

"A therapist should be knowledgeable about the many self-help books available on phobias and panic. I went to several before finding an expert who knew exactly what would be helpful to read on my own while working along with the group program."

"My therapist understood how I felt, but didn't help me understand why I react as I do. He never offered suggestions on how to manage my phobia."

"One therapist made me feel like I needed major analysis for a long time. In fact, I saw him for five years and he never once said that I had agoraphobia. One said that all I needed was to learn to relax and that would solve my problem. When I asked him if I would go crazy or have a heart attack or die, he said that one couldn't guarantee that one wouldn't have a heart attack. That wasn't very reassuring."

"I saw two doctors before finding TERRAP. Neither gave me any insight about what I had or how to get better. I was on the verge of suicide."

* * *

In working with phobics and panic victims who have been disabled for years by their disorder, we have a dual reaction to them reaching recovery. We share their elation at the dramatic changes they make in their ability to function, as they put it, "like a normal person." However, there is a sense of sadness over the years that have been lost before that patient began the steps to recovery. If only they had been connected with the most effective treatment for recovery before the disorder took over their lives and the lives of their families.

As a therapist, you are in the all-important position of diagnosing your patient, educating them about the disorder you have identified, and putting them in touch with a comprehensive treatment program to alleviate anxiety and improve daily functioning. By doing so, you reassure this very anxious patient of the following:

a. There is a name for their disorder
b. They are not "going crazy"
c. There are many others who have been victimized by this disorder
d. There is specific, comprehensive, effective treatment for their disorder
e. You will put them in touch with that specific treatment
f. You will continue to support them in their efforts toward recovery

You will serve your patient best by providing this light at the end of the tunnel.

2. Be Familiar with the DSM-III-R Diagnoses for Panic Disorder, Agoraphobia, and Other Anxiety Disorders.

For your convenience, the diagnostic criteria for panic disorder, agoraphobia, and other related anxiety disorders is provided on pages 132 to 136. This information is especially helpful in differential diagnosis. You may even choose to read selected sections of the diagnostic criteria aloud to your patient to elicit more information on features that do and do not apply to the clinical picture. Information concerning the cognitive and experiential components of the disorder may be gathered by asking specific questions such as:

a. Is it difficult for you to be alone?
b. Do you have a fear of losing control? Do you find yourself avoiding places from which escape may be difficult?
c. Do you have a feeling of unreality during these attacks?

The patient's answers to these and other questions will help clarify diagnosis of an anxiety disorder.

Keep in mind that additional diagnoses may apply to your patient—for example, depression, adjustment disorder, dysthymic disorder, or marital problems. However, while all of these diagnoses require therapeutic intervention, it is important to establish the disabling features of the anxiety disorder as the *first priority* for intervention. Just as the battered woman's broken leg is attended to before family intervention is attempted, so should the panic victim's symptomatology and deficits in functioning be addressed as a first step. Once the patient's anxiety is reduced and they are performing daily activities more successfully, they can shift their focus from their body to issues of importance related to the generation and maintenance of such a disorder. The therapist working with this patient on these specific issues will reach treatment goals faster once the patient's anxiety is eliminated as a distraction.

3. Be Aware of the Most Comprehensive Treatment for Anxiety Disorders.

By thoroughly reading chapter 2, you will gain the following: (a) an understanding of comprehensive treatment for these disorders, (b) information on how to locate and refer to such a program of treatment, and (c) answers to questions panic victims most often ask regarding treatment. All of this information will enable you to better explain routes to recovery for the victim, and, thereby, provide helpful direction.

4. Acknowledge the Necessity for Specialized Treatment.

All responsible professionals acknowledge the value and necessity of specialized treatment when appropriate. All competent therapists seeing an alcoholic patient will encourage that patient's involvement in Alcoholics Anonymous. Similarly, therapists who first see an obese smoker with a history of stroke will urge that patient's involvement in a group program of weight loss and smoking cessation while exploring reasons for self-defeating behavior in individual sessions.

The panic disorder, agoraphobic, and other phobic patients require specialized treatment just as the alcoholic, the anorexic, or the patient experiencing sexual dysfunction requires specialized treatment. The agoraphobic or panic disorder patient whose therapist is not familiar with Dr. Claire Weekes's books or other self-help books for the panic victim is not seeing a specialist in these disorders. The therapist who does not use a consulting psychiatrist to evaluate the appropriateness of medication is not a specialist in these disorders. And the therapist who is not able to instruct the patient in anxiety control techniques, arrange in vivo desensitization sessions, or provide the patient with a panic disorder or agoraphobic peer group is not a specialist in these disorders. Patients involved with such therapists will lose time in their recovery process by not learning the tools so necessary for improvement.

Of course, the patient who is involved with a comprehensive program of treatment and is also able to explore individual issues of importance in one-to-one sessions is best served. These sessions can be provided by an affiliate of the comprehensive program, or another therapist familiar with issues of importance to the typical panic victim. However, it is both helpful and necessary for these various therapists to be in close, positive touch with one another to best coordinate the treatment plan for the panic victim.

5. Be Available to Explore Issues Raised Through Comprehensive Treatment.

Anxiety disorder patients who have completed a comprehensive program of treatment are in the best position to pursue individual issues that may have contributed to, or maintained their disorders. With their anxiety under control, and the improvement in their everyday functioning, these patients are now able to shift their focus to the specific issues they must address to maintain gains made in treatment:

a. the mother whose only child was killed in a car accident must recognize and work through her anger
b. the young man who feels overwhelmed by financial stress and impending fatherhood must allow himself to express his "what ifs," and to work with these fears productively
c. a woman who feels trapped in a loveless marriage where there is emotional and physical abuse must explore options to continuing in this stressful situation

In these and other cases, the anxiety the patient has experienced has served a purpose. It has prevented him or her from facing thoughts, feelings, and decisions that are particularly frightening to acknowledge and to act on productively. For example:

a. the grieving mother who has been taught never to question her religion learns that the anger she feels toward a God who could let such a thing happen has been converted to anxiety and panic

b. the young man who is experiencing the ambivalence and "what ifs" of most new fathers-to-be learns that his fears do not make him less of a man, just more human

c. the woman entrapped in an abusive marriage learns that her previous inability to be alone is no longer an excuse to expose herself and her children to domestic violence

As part of a comprehensive treatment program, your patient will become aware of the most typical issues underlying the continuation of many disorders of panic:

unresolved grief, incomplete individuation, unexpressed anger, fear of abandonment, a history of physical or emotional abuse or other trauma, perfectionism, an inability to forgive others for past transgressions, difficulty trusting others, and rigidity of thinking.

While these issues may have been addressed in a general way within a group format, most patients come away from comprehensive treatment understanding the specific issues they need to explore individually. They are also aware of other sources that can be helpful to their recovery—i.e., Alanon, an Adult Children of Alcoholics group, or a vocational testing center to assist the agoraphobic now able to take a part-time job. Various readings relating to issues of importance will have also been recommended by a comprehensive treatment program.

Most patients completing a comprehensive program within a group format are advised to pursue individual, marital, or family therapy to maintain or improve gains they have made. While some patients elect to stop treat-

ment when their symptomatology is no longer an obstacle
to everyday functioning, the majority of patients *do* pursue
additional therapy. Therefore, if you have referred an
anxiety patient for comprehensive treatment, the patient
will likely return to you asymptomatic, and eager to start
work on specific areas of personal interest.

**6. Become More Familiar with Literature Available on
Panic Disorder and Agoraphobia.**

   While you will not be treating your patient directly for
these disorders, it will be helpful to gain insight into the
experimential component of the disorders as well as treatment issues of relevance. There are several excellent books
on these subjects listed in the Suggested Readings section
at the end of this book. It will be especially helpful for you
to gain insight on the life-style adjustments of panic victims, and the systems approach stressed in the ongoing
treatment of these disorders. Your patients will appreciate
your understanding of what they have experienced and
the anxiety management tools they must use on a daily
basis.
   As you become more familiar with the recommended
treatments for these disorders, be careful that you do not
use your improved understanding to rationalize a failure
to refer a patient to a comprehensive program of treatment. Use this information to help patients involved in or
completing such a program. For example, patients may
avoid discussion of anxiety-provoking topics just as they
avoided places and situations associated with anxiety when
they were more symptomatic. The recommended books
will aid you in gently confronting your patient on this new
kind of avoidance paradigm. The role of the therapist
here would be to encourage the patient to confront per-

sonal areas of stress (a troubled marriage, difficulty with intimacy, asserting feelings of anger or disappointment) as conscientiously as they confronted their anxiety disorder.

7. Educate Your Local Professional Society about Specialized Referral Sources for the Anxiety Disorder Patient.

Most professionals are eager to learn about good referral sources in areas where they lack expertise. Many therapists feel frustrated when they are able to identify a disabling disorder, but are unaware of comprehensive treatment programs for such disorders. The local professional society or organization is a forum in which various disorders and sources of specialized treatment can be discussed and identified. You might consider asking a TERRAP provider or a staff member of another comprehensive treatment program to give a presentation on panic disorder and agoraphobia and the treatment strategies employed with these disorders. Such an individual could help you and your colleagues with questions you might have on differential diagnosis and how best to help such patients.

8. Locate and Refer to Comprehensive Treatment Programs in Your Area.

We recommend that you contact your nearest teaching hospital or university to learn of any comprehensive program they offer for panic disorder, agoraphobia, and simple phobias. We also recommend contacting the national office of the TERRAP Phobia Program. This organization will give you the name of the provider and location nearest you. Since TERRAP is a nationally offered program, there are branches in all fifty states. One may be an appropriate distance for referral. If so, it is recommended that you call that provider to receive TERRAP materials to better acquaint you with the program. It will also be helpful to establish a personal contact with this specialist so that you feel more comfortable making a referral.

The Phobia Society of America can send you a national directory of providers for anxiety disorders. It can also, by telephone, give you the locations of treatment services closest to you. Keep in mind that not all providers listed in this directory provide comprehensive treatment. It is best to contact the providers within your referral area to learn about their particular program of treatment. Refer to chapter 2 ("Step Two: Be Aware of the Most Comprehensive Treatment for Recovery," pages 56 to 57) to assess the comprehensiveness of each provider's treatment program.

9. Know Your Options If No Comprehensive Treatment Program Is Available in Your Area.

If you have verified that there is no comprehensive treatment program in your area, the following options are available to you:

a. The TERRAP Phobia Program has an excellent correspondence course for panic victims unable to reach a treatment group. This program consists of comprehensive reading materials, instruction in helpful techniques for anxiety reduction, and tape recordings of TERRAP sessions to give the patient a sense of group inclusion. The recipient of the correspondence course is also able to have telephone contact (clarification, support, suggestions) with the staff of the TERRAP organization.

Further information on the correspondence course is available by contacting the TERRAP organization: (TERRAP Phobia Programs, 648 Menlo Avenue #5, Menlo Park, California 94025. Telephone: (415) 327-1312; (1-800) 2-PHOBIA).

b. Investigate becoming a TERRAP provider in your area. This may be explored by contacting the TERRAP organization in Menlo Park, California. Providers selected as TERRAP staff are trained in all treatment techniques of this comprehensive program by current TERRAP providers and are supervised by the TERRAP director for that state.

c. Become more familiar with panic disorder and agoraphobia through the various readings suggested in the Suggested Readings section at the conclusion of this book, and recommend those appropriate for your patients. *Your Phobia* by Zane and Milt is especially helpful in explaining the clinical, experiential, and treatment aspects of these disorders. They provide additional information on how the patient can conduct practice sessions with the aid of a "helper," as well as how to organize a mutual support group.

d. Investigate nearby providers listed in the directory of the Phobia Society of America who offer programs that, while not necessarily comprehensive, contain many of the elements of such a program. Contact these providers and evaluate the quality of such a program by referring to chapter 2 ("Step Two: Be Aware of the Most Comprehensive Treatment for Recovery," pages 56 to 57). Remember that the key elements of treatment are those of the availability of practice sessions, peer group involvement, instruction in behavioral and cognitive techniques of anxiety management, and evaluation for medication.

e. Take advantage of national organizations and newsletters in the field of anxiety disorders. Join the Phobia Society of America for a nominal fee, and gain access to the latest research and literature on anxiety disorders through that organization's newsletter. The society also holds yearly national conferences offering presentations and workshops by recognized experts in this field. The *TERRAP Times* is another informative newsletter for the professional and the recovering victim of panic. Subscription information is outlined in chapter 2.

5

How the Physician (or Health Care Professional) Can Help

While this chapter is addressed primarily to the physician, nurse, or other health care worker, it will be of value to the spouse, friend, and even the panic sufferer as well. Many panic victims are anxious about discussing their disorder with a physician, particularly those components that are not medically related, such as fear of losing control. Use this section to learn more about the physician's role in dealing with panic patients, including what is most helpful for the victim and the physician to discuss with each other. Many panic victims help educate their doctors to the thoughts, feelings, and experiences of their disorder. And those doctors are grateful for this insight since it helps them to be more sensitive to the fears and needs of panic victims. Here, it will be helpful for the victim and other support people to learn more about the medical focus of these disorders and the role the physician can best play to facilitate recovery.

Here is a list of the points encompassing the physician's role to be discussed in this chapter:

1. Recognize the all-important role you play in diagnosing the disorder and paving the road to comprehensive treatment.

2. Be familiar with the DSM-III-R diagnoses for panic disorder with and without agoraphobia, and other related anxiety disorders.
3. Explore possible physical causes for the reported symptomatology.
4. Be aware of the most comprehensive treatment for recovery.
5. Recognize the necessity of referring your patient to a panic disorder and phobia specialist.
6. Discuss the diagnosis fully with the patient.
7. Convince your patient of the need for specialized treatment for their disorder.
8. Locate and refer to comprehensive treatment programs in your area.
9. Reassure your patient as to the physical effects of anxiety and panic attacks.
10. Consider the patient's caffeine intake as contributory to anxiety.
11. Check for alcohol or other drug abuse as self-medication for the disorder.
12. Learn from your patient about the disorder and what they request from a physician.
13. Educate your local medical group or society about comprehensive treatment sources for these disorders.
14. Alert emergency room physicians to comprehensive treatment sources for these disorders.

1. Recognize the All-important Role You Play in Diagnosing the Disorder and Paving the Road to Comprehensive Treatment.

You may very well be the first professional to see the phobic or panic victim. The first panic attack of these disorders almost always results in the victim's fearing for his or her health. Many are sure that they are having a heart attack or other health emergency. Consequently, the first stop made by most panic victims is their local emergency room, the office of their family physician, or some other medical specialist.

Ballenger et al. (1987) discusses that while the prevalence of panic disorder is between three percent to seven percent in the general population, many of these patients remain unrecognized in primary care, internal medicine, and cardiology practices. The over ninety percent of panic disorder patients who believe they have a physical disorder present not to psychiatrists or psychologists, but instead to neurologists (forty-four percent), cardiologists (thirty-nine percent), and gastroenterologists (thirty-three percent). Ballenger et al. (1987) estimates that as many as one-third of patients presenting with atypical chest pain, particularly those with normal coronary angiogram results, have unrecognized panic disorder.

Since the victim is coming to you for the answer to the question, "What is happening to me?" it is extremely important that you be familiar with points of differential diagnosis, the disorder itself, treatment strategies, and the availability of comprehensive treatment in your area.

2. Be Familiar with the DSM-III-R Diagnoses for Panic Disorder with and without Agoraphobia, and Other Related Anxiety Disorders.

For your convenience, the diagnostic criteria for panic disorder with and without agoraphobia, and other related anxiety disorders is provided on pages 132 to 136.

This information is particularly helpful in differential diagnosis. A physician may even choose to read selected sections of the diagnostic criteria aloud to the patient to elicit more information on features that do and do not

Diagnostic criteria for Panic Disorder

A. At some time during the disturbance, one or more panic attacks (discrete periods of intense fear or discomfort) have occurred that were (1) unexpected, i.e., did not occur immediately before or on exposure to a situation that almost always caused anxiety, and (2) not triggered by situations in which the person was the focus of others' attention.

B. Either four attacks, as defined in criterion A, have occurred within a four-week period, or one or more attacks have been followed by a period of at least a month of persistent fear of having another attack.

C. At least four of the following symptoms developed during at least one of the attacks:

   (1) shortness of breath (dyspnea) or smothering sensations
   (2) dizziness, unsteady feelings, or faintness
   (3) palpitations or accelerated heart rate (tachycardia)
   (4) trembling or shaking
   (5) sweating
   (6) choking
   (7) nausea or abdominal distress
   (8) depersonalization or derealization
   (9) numbness or tingling sensations (paresthesias)
 (10) flushes (hot flashes) or chills
 (11) chest pain or discomfort
 (12) fear of dying
 (13) fear of going crazy or of doing something uncontrolled

Note: Attacks involving four or more symptoms are panic attacks; attacks involving fewer than four symptoms are limited symptom attacks (see Agoraphobia without History of Panic Disorder, p. 135).

D. During at least some of the attacks, at least four of the C symptoms developed suddenly and increased in intensity within ten minutes of the beginning of the first C symptom noticed in the attack.

E. It cannot be established that an organic factor initiated and maintained the disturbance, e.g., Amphetamine or Caffeine Intoxication, hyperthyroidism.

Note: Mitral valve prolapse may be an associated condition, but does not preclude a diagnosis of Panic Disorder.

Types of Panic Disorder

Diagnostic criteria for 300.21 Panic Disorder with Agoraphobia

A. Meets the criteria for Panic Disorder.

B. Agoraphobia: Fear of being in places or situations from which escape might be difficult (or embarrassing) or in which help might not be available in the event of a panic attack. (Include cases in which persistent avoidance behavior originated during an active phase of Panic Disorder, even if the person does not attribute the avoidance behavior to fear of having a panic attack.) As a result of this fear, the person either restricts travel or needs a companion when away from home, or else endures agoraphobic situations despite intense anxiety. Common agoraphobic situations include being outside the home alone, being in a crowd or standing in a line, being on a bridge, and traveling in a bus, train, or car.

Specify current severity of agoraphobic avoidance:

Mild: Some avoidance (or endurance with distress), but relatively normal life-style, e.g., travels unaccompanied when necessary, such as to work or to shop; otherwise avoids traveling alone.

Moderate: Avoidance results in constricted life-style, e.g., the person is able to leave the house alone, but not to go more than a few miles unaccompanied.

Severe: Avoidance results in being nearly or completely housebound or unable to leave the house unaccompanied.

In Partial Remission: No current agoraphobic avoidance, but some agoraphobic avoidance during the past six months.

In Full Remission: No current agoraphobic avoidance and none during the past six months.

Specify current severity of panic attacks:

Mild: During the past month, either all attacks have been limited symptom attacks (i.e., fewer than four symptoms), or there has been no more than one panic attack.

Moderate: During the past month attacks have been intermediate between "mild" and "severe."

Severe: During the past month, there have been at least eight panic attacks.

In Partial Remission: The condition has been intermediate between "In Full Remission" and "Mild."

In Full Remission: During the past six months, there have been no panic or limited symptom attacks.

Diagnostic criteria for 300.01 Panic Disorder without Agoraphobia

A. Meets the criteria for Panic Disorder.

B. Absence of Agoraphobia, as defined above.

Specify current severity of panic attacks, as defined above.

Diagnostic criteria for 300.22 Agoraphobia without History of Panic Disorder

A. Agoraphobia: Fear of being in places or situations from which escape might be difficult (or embarrassing) or in which help might not be available in the event of suddenly developing a symptom(s) that could be incapacitating or extremely embarrassing. Examples include: dizziness or falling, depersonalization or derealization, loss of bladder or bowel control, vomiting, or cardiac distress. As a result of this fear, the person either restricts travel or needs a companion when away from home, or else endures agoraphobic situations despite intense anxiety. Common agoraphobic situations include being outside the home alone, being in a crowd or standing in a line, being on a bridge, and traveling in a bus, train, or car.

B. Has never met the criteria for Panic Disorder.

Specify with or without limited symptom attacks.

Diagnostic criteria for 300.23 Social Phobia

A. A persistent fear of one or more situations (the social phobic situations) in which the person is exposed to possible scrutiny by others and fears that he or she may do something or act in a way that will be humiliating or embarrassing. Examples include: being unable to continue talking while speaking in public, choking on food when eating in front of others, being unable to urinate in a public lavatory, hand-trembling when writing in the presence of others, and saying foolish things or not being able to answer questions in social situations.

B. If an Axis III or another Axis I disorder is present, the fear in A is unrelated to it, e.g., the fear is not of having a panic attack (Panic Disorder), stuttering (Stuttering), trembling (Parkinson's disease), or exhibiting abnormal eating behavior (Anorexia Nervosa or Bulimia Nervosa).

C. During some phase of the disturbance, exposure to the specific phobic stimulus (or stimuli) almost invariably provokes an immediate anxiety response.

D. The phobic situation(s) is avoided, or is endured with intense anxiety.

E. The avoidant behavior interferes with occupational functioning or with usual social activities or relationships with others, or there is marked distress about having the fear.

F. The person recognizes that his or her fear is excessive or unreasonable.

G. If the person is under 18, the disturbance does not meet the criteria for Avoidant Disorder of Childhood or Adolescence.

Specify generalized type if the phobic situation includes most social situations, and also consider the additional diagnosis of Avoidant Personality Disorder.

Diagnostic criteria for 300.29 Simple Phobia

A. A persistent fear of a circumscribed stimulus (object or situation) other than fear of having a panic attack (as in Panic Disorder) or of humiliation or embarrassment in certain social situations (as in Social Phobia).

Note: Do not include fears that are part of Panic Disorder with Agoraphobia or Agoraphobia without History of Panic Disorder.

B. During some phase of the disturbance, exposure to the specific phobic stimulus (or stimuli) almost invariably provokes an immediate anxiety response.

apply to that patient's clinical picture. In this way, there is a holistic approach to the evaluation of the physical symptomatology.

Often patients will be more likely to discuss only the physical features of their disorder with their physicians. The physician familiar with the diagnostic criteria for the major anxiety disorders can elicit information concerning the cognitive, experiential, and behavioral components of the disorder as well by asking specific questions such as:

- Is it difficult for you to be alone?
- Do you have a fear of losing control?
- Do you find yourself avoiding places from which escape may be difficult?
- Do you have a feeling of unreality during these attacks?

The patient's answers to these and other questions will help clarify diagnosis of an anxiety disorder.

Your role as physician, then, is to establish whether the patient's disorder is a *physical* disorder with accompanying psychological symptoms, or is a *mental* disorder with accompanying physical symptoms. Obviously, this is of paramount importance in treatment planning and referral.

3. Explore Possible Physical Causes for the Reported Symptomatology.

Many of our patients have been referred to us by their physicians. Referral has followed comprehensive medical evaluation to rule out any medical condition that would explain the presenting symptoms or further contribute to the clinical picture. It is not uncommon that these patients have been evaluated by their family physicians, emergency room physicians, cardiologists, endocrinologists, and other medical specialists. They have usually been evaluated for cardiac disorders, thyroid irregularities, substance abuse, inner ear disorders, hypoglycemia, and even premenstrual syndrome.

Ballenger et al. (1987) lists the following physical conditions that may mimic symptoms of panic disorder:

a. Caffeinism
b. Illicit drug use (amphetamines, cocaine, marijuana, or alcohol or sedative withdrawal)
c. Endocrine disorders
   1. Hyperthyroidism
   2. Hypoglycemia
   3. Multiple endocrine adenomata
   4. Pheochromocytoma
   5. Hypoparathyroidism
   6. Cushing's syndrome
d. Cardiovascular disorders
   1. Angina pectoris
   2. Paroxysmal atrial tachycardia
   3. Mitral valve prolapse
e. Respiratory distress
   1. Asthma
   2. Chronic obstructive pulmonary disease
   3. Pulmonary embolus
f. Drug intoxication (e.g., aminophylline, ephedrine, digitalis, antidepressants, etc.)
g. Neurologic disorders (partial complex seizures)
h. Cerebrovascular disorders (transient ischemic attacks)
i. Menopause
j. Anemia

Each of the preceding conditions varies in the degree to which it may be confused with panic disorder. Ballenger et al. (1987) stresses the importance of diagnostic differentiation through careful history taking, physical examination, and laboratory testing. He also discusses recent research on various conditions and their relationship to panic disorder, e.g., hypoglycemia (anxiety from this disorder does not appear involved in the anxiety and panic of the panic disorder patient), and mitral valve prolapse (while thirty percent to fifty percent of panic disorder patients and agoraphobic patients have mitral valve prolapse, patients with mitral valve prolapse do not have a higher incidence of panic disorder than that of the general population. Additionally, panic disorder patients with mitral valve prolapse experience the same success in treatment as the non-mitral valve prolapse panic disorder patient).

A routine workup with panic disorder patients to explore the involvement of any of the preceding conditions usually includes the following (Ballenger et al., 1987):

1. *A symptomatic history* focusing on symptomatology of panic attacks and phobias (onset and length of symptoms, qualitative description of symptoms, family history of any anxiety disorder, or other condition with related symptomatology).
2. *A drug history* focusing upon caffeine use and drug use to assess intoxication and withdrawal involvement.
3. *A general medical history* focusing on disorders of the cardiac, endocrine, and neurologic systems.
4. *A physical examination* for detection of cardiac arrhythmias or murmurs, palpable thyroid, suggestions of thyroid disease, systematic hypertension, and respiratory disorder.
5. *Laboratory examination* involving a complete blood count, electrolytes, calcium, phosphorus, T3, T4, and a drug screening if appropriate.

In the ideal situation, the panic patient who is comprehensively evaluated medically to rule out physical systems etiology is referred for comprehensive psychological treatment. We are always pleased to interview these patients for our program since it saves the step of referring them for medical evaluation. We routinely refer new patients to their family physician or an internist known to us to rule out a medical disorder as the generator of their symptomatology before accepting them for our treatment program, and any competent panic specialist will do the same.

4. Be Aware of the Most Comprehensive Treatment for Recovery.

For a complete discussion and locations of comprehensive treatment for recovery, we refer you to chapter 2, specifically the sections labeled "Step Two" and "Step Three" (pages 56 to 61). A summary of comprehensive recovery methods and programs is presented here.

Experts in the field of anxiety disorders agree that the most effective treatment for panic disorder, agoraphobia, and other similar anxiety disorders involves a combination of behavior therapy, cognitive therapy, education, group support, and medication as appropriate. This is the standard, currently recommended practice offered at most teaching hospitals, and universities including such nationally known treatment centers as the White Plains Hospital Phobia Clinic (White Plains, New York), the TERRAP Phobia Program (Menlo Park, California), Roundhouse Square Psychiatric Center (Alexandria, Virginia), and Temple University Agoraphobia and Anxiety Center (Bala Cynwyd, Pennsylvania). Such programs are usually staffed with psychologists, psychiatrists, social workers, and other mental health professionals. They may also utilize recovering patients to serve as role models for panic victims entering a treatment program.

The best comprehensive treatment programs usually include the following components:

a. *Time-limited treatment groups* (usually eight to sixteen weeks) which meet weekly
b. *Instruction in anxiety disorders and the reduction of anxiety* (instruction in the measurement and recording of symptoms, relaxation training, stress reduction training, cognitive coping strategies, written materials)
c. *In vivo, systematic desensitization sessions*—sessions where a staff member accompanies the patient in entering difficult situations in a step-by-step way (for example, grocery stores, driving, staying alone, separating in a mall, standing in lines, using elevators, crossing bridges)
d. *Evaluation for medication* as appropriate by an affiliated psychiatrist
e. *Instruction in and discussion of related issues of importance* for anxiety disorder patients (assertiveness, unresolved grief, incomplete individuation, self-esteem, perfectionism, rigidity of thinking, pessimism, feelings of powerlessness)
f. *An informational session conducted for the family and close support people of the panic victim* providing clarity about the disorder and their role in helping the victim
g. *Journal keeping* (documentation of thoughts, feelings, behavior, practice sessions, progress, and setbacks) that provides insight to the patient and patient monitoring for the therapist
h. *Homework assignments* (readings both directly and indirectly related to the disorder, for example, Claire Weekes's books, assertiveness readings, practice assignments for extending limits with a practice partner)
i. *Follow-up support groups and individual psychotherapy* as needed to enhance recovery and address individual issues

The TERRAP Phobia Program (an acronym for territorial apprehensiveness) is a nationwide, standardized program of treatment that includes *all* of the components previously outlined. Providers of this program are usually psychologists or social workers who have had extensive training and experience in the recommended multimodal program of recovery. These TERRAP therapists are usually independently based therapists with consulting psychiatrists for medication evaluation. As experienced providers of the TERRAP program, we acknowledge our bias in recommending this very comprehensive and successful program, if available in your area.

The TERRAP program is currently the only *nationally* available standardized program for anxiety disorders that is professionally administered. This is especially important for anxiety-disorder patients who do not live near medical centers, or university-based treatment programs. Another advantage of the TERRAP program is that the staff of TERRAP is selected, trained, and supervised by the national and state directors of TERRAP, assuring uniformity and quality control of treatment.

Additional specialized treatment sources, both comprehensive and limited may be explored by contacting the Phobia Society of America (PSA). This national clearinghouse of information and referral sources can provide you with all of the treatment sources in your area. We recommend using the comprehensive services listing to evaluate the most effective treatment for your patients. (See pages 58 to 61 for information on contacting TERRAP and the Phobia Society of America.)

5. Recognize the Necessity of Referring Your Patient to a Panic Disorder and Phobia Specialist.

All responsible, ethical professionals acknowledge their areas of expertise and their areas of limitation. That is the reason the cardiologist refers a head trauma patient to a neurologist. It is the reason that when a first-time patient presents to us with an eating disorder we refer him or her to a specialized program of treatment for that very complicated disorder.

It is a fact, however, that most prescriptions for benzodiazepines are written by nonpsychiatric physicians. Couple this with the fact that antianxiety medications, particularly benzodiazepines, are the most frequently prescribed medications in recent history (Hollister, 1980). This information makes a powerful statement regarding the prevalence of clinically significant anxiety presented in medical settings, as well as the tendency for the nonpsychiatric physician to supervise the psychotropic medications for their patients (Ballenger et al., 1987).

You may typically refer patients requiring psychotherapy of any kind to an excellent therapist in your area. However, as competent as this therapist may be, if he or she is not a trained specialist in comprehensive panic and phobia treatment, your patient will not be receiving the best referral from you.

The advantage of referring to a specialized program or specialist is threefold:

1. Your patient will receive the comprehensive treatment recognized to be the most effective, including access to evaluation for the most appropriate medication.
2. These will be the professionals who can provide your patient with a peer group experiencing similar symptoms, thoughts, feelings, and behavior. Experts in this field recognize the tremendous importance of this professionally supervised group-support aspect of treatment. This is the best and the most direct way to help your patient understand that:
   a. I am not alone. (Here are other people like me.)

     b. I am not "going crazy." (These other people have the same thing I have, and they're not crazy!)

     c. It's all right to talk about what I'm thinking and feeling. (These people will understand.)

Remember how comforting (not to mention therapeutic!) it was to talk with other medical students, residents, and physicians studying for the various exams you had to take? Remember how good it felt to learn that you weren't the only one having anxiety about passing? It's the same experience the infertile couple is provided when they meet other similar couples and get a chance to commiserate and learn from each other and support each other. There is no substitute for this group experience in overcoming disability: witness the success of Alcoholics Anonymous, and the Weight Watchers program. While the professional can provide the basic treatment needed for recovery, only the peer can provide the comfort and moral support that comes with identification.

3. Panic and phobia specialists will be the professionals in a position to conduct in vivo desensitization treatment with your patient. This means that the patient who is terrified of entering a grocery store will be accompanied to a grocery store by a therapist according to a prearranged hierarchy of exposure. It means that the man terrified of driving more than two miles from his home will be able to extend his driving limits with the help of a therapist sitting right next to him in the car, or following him in another car with a citizen-band radio to extend limits even further. It means that the woman terrified of staying alone in her home can practice being alone with her therapist leaving that house for seconds at a time, then minutes at a time, then hours at a time with telephone contact.

     No matter how compassionate, knowledgeable, or insightful a therapist may be in dealing with an agoraphobia victim, if that patient is not being helped directly to reenter anxiety-provoking situations, that patient's specific needs are not fully met.

While many excellent therapists have the training to conduct such sessions, they may be unable to leave their offices to do so. A specialist in this field will have the kind of professional practice that enables this desensitization process.

6. Discuss the Diagnosis Fully with the Patient.

This assumes that you feel comfortable in making a firm diagnosis of an anxiety disorder. If you are sure that the disorder is not typically medical in nature, but it is unclear which specific anxiety disorder is present, you may feel comfortable in consulting a specialist in this field for input on specific diagnosis. (Information on how to locate such a specialist in your area is provided in chapter 2 under "Step Three: Locate a Program of Comprehensive Treatment," pages 58 to 61).

Many patients become alarmed when told that no physical cause for their symptomatology is evident. While the physician may feel that this is comforting information, it often has the opposite effect on patients. They report feeling even more frightened than they were upon entering the physician's office with their mysterious disorder. Hearing that there is no physical cause for what they are experiencing is usually perceived by the patients or communicated to them as "Everything is fine." The patients are now totally confused and more worried than before since they know they are *not* fine, and that something is *very* wrong. Additionally, they now feel more alone in their anguish since the cause for their symptomatology remains a mystery.

There is a danger of "dropping the ball" at this point in

your contact with the patient. Be aware that even while you attempt to reassure your patient that his or her health is "fine," that this finding may *add* feelings of frustration and depression to your patient's presenting symptom of panic. Many of these patients will have come to you with strong hopes and expectations of discovering a concrete, simple, "fixable" basis for their symptoms.

You must not drop the ball, or dead-end treatment by reassuring them about what they *don't* have while neglecting to educate them about what they *do* have. Specifically, you should say, "What you *don't* have is a heart problem. What you *do* have is an anxiety disorder called (fill in the blank). It is stress-related, it is treatable, and there is comprehensive treatment that I can put you in touch with."

You will find that labeling the disorder for the patient will somehow reassure him or her that it is more manageable, and, thereby, less frightening. The patient reasons, "If there's a name for it, then I can't be the only one who has it, and there must be a way to recover from it. What a relief!"

7. Convince Your Patient of the Need for Specialized Treatment for Their Disorder.

This may be very difficult. Even if you are the most compassionate authority on anxiety treatment, your patient may refuse to follow through on your referral. Why? In a word, fear. The fear of starting something new. The fear of change. Add this fear to this type of patient's tendency to avoid any situation evoking anxiety. Regardless of how disabling their disorder, many victims refuse to get help simply because it feels so safe to stay with the familiar way of dealing with the disorder.

Your goal is to convince your patients of the following:

1. The anxiety disorder will, most likely, not improve without intervention. Indeed, it may worsen.
2. There is effective, comprehensive treatment for their disorder.
3. They are not alone in their struggle with the disorder.
4. They are not "going crazy," a primary fear of the victim. Panic disorder, agoraphobia, and other phobias do not, even in their most severe stages lead to psychosis, or a break with reality.
5. They should consider getting this specialized help as seriously as they would if it were a life-threatening disorder. (Clarify that while these disorders are not *literally* life threatening, that they threaten the victim's preferred life-style and independence.)
6. They should consider the effects of their disorder upon the family, and the ramifications of not helping themselves to recovery.
7. Comprehensive treatment is effective, short-term, and will involve meeting others like themselves to provide comfort and support.
8. Treatment is not panic inducing. It is rigorous and demanding, but also enlightening, liberating, and even fun.
9. Symptomatic relief provided by medication is usually a temporary solution to an ongoing problem. While medication can be helpful in some instances, it is most effective in conjunction with a comprehensive program of recovery.
10. You will monitor their progress in a program of recovery and continue to treat them for disorders more within your areas of specialty.
11. They owe it to themselves and their family to make the first step toward recovery by contacting a treatment source (your referral) to become more comfortable with the idea of entering comprehensive treatment.

In cases where you feel the patient is extremely fearful of the disorder and the idea of comprehensive treatment, we recommend that you advise them to read Dr. Claire Weekes's *Hope and Help for Your Nerves* and/or *Peace from Nervous Suffering*. Both are highly respected, tremendously informative, and comforting books for the panic victim. These books are in paperback and can be located in the self-help section of any good bookstore. Most panic victims find tremendous reassurance in the Weekes books. Many credit Dr. Weekes's warm, informative style with enabling them to see professional treatment as less frightening. This enabled them to take that first step toward recovery.

8. Locate and Refer to Comprehensive Treatment Programs in Your Area.

We refer you to chapter 2 for the addresses and phone numbers of The Phobia Society of America, and the national office of the TERRAP Phobia Program (See "Step Three: Locate a Program of Comprehensive Treatment," pages 58 to 61). After locating the most comprehensive treatment sources in your area, call your nearby provider to receive materials acquainting you with that specific program of treatment. It will also be helpful to establish a personal contact with this specialist so that you feel more comfortable making a referral to that source. We advise that you thoroughly familiarize yourself with any program or specialist to which you refer.

You may find that comprehensive programs of treatment are too far away from you to serve as realistic referral sources. In this case, you may consider one of the less-comprehensive programs of treatment listed in the Phobia Society of America directory that is closer to your area.

Keep in mind that the most important components of treatment are those of the availability of practice sessions, peer-group involvement, instruction in behavioral and cognitive techniques of anxiety management, and evaluation for medication. Regardless of the referral source you choose, we recommend seeking more information about that specific source before referral.

9. Reassure Your Patient as to the Physical Effects of Anxiety and Panic Attacks.

Most panic victims want to know the answers to the following questions: Can I have a heart attack from a panic attack? Will continual episodes of panic and anxiety wear down my system and threaten my life? Of course the answers they want to hear are the following: No, you cannot die from a panic attack. No, there are no cumulative negative effects on your health from anxiety and panic. As a responsible professional, however, you are unable to be so simplistic and absolute. You need to address this very delicate set of questions in such a way that the patient is reassured yet also educated as to when to have the symptoms medically evaluated. This will require tactful wording of information that is within your professional domain rather than ours. However, we can prepare you for the probability that your patient may seek repeated reassurance that the risk of danger from panic is minimal. (Most are reassured to learn that even in the midst of a panic attack, results of the physical examination and electrocardiogram are generally normal or show only a sinus tachycardia [Ballenger et al., 1987].) Obviously, each patient should be addressed as an individual case based upon age, health status, and any preexisting medical disorders.

In rare cases, patients experiencing panic may become

extremely needy and demanding of their physicians. One young man called his family physician several times a week to be reassured that he was not dying when experiencing a panic attack. He had also logged over forty trips a year to various emergency rooms when experiencing panic. While undergoing extensive testing each time he was admitted to any emergency room, this man had developed a reputation among area physicians for "crying wolf." This raises the very important point that, while a patient may have a history of symptoms diagnosed as panic-related, the possibility that those symptoms *could* be medically related—for example, a heart attack—should *not* be automatically ruled out based upon past history. For example, a review of panic disorder patients at the National Institute of Mental Health found that fifty-eight percent of those patients had previously unrecognized and undiagnosed medical conditions that involved multiple systems but were apparently unrelated to the panic attacks themselves (Uhde and Maser, 1985).

10. Consider the Patient's Caffeine Intake as Contributory to Anxiety.

Many of the patients with whom we have worked have had a long history of general anxiety before the onset of their panic disorder or agoraphobia. Several have attempted to "self-medicate" through coffee or tea consumption. Most were unaware of the connection between their use of caffeine and their feelings of anxiety or anxiety relief. They just knew that they needed a cup of coffee or tea to calm them down at times.

Research conducted at the National Institute of Mental Health suggested that panic-disorder patients are more reactive to caffeine than are nonpanic patients. Additionally, in a self-report survey, these panic-disorder patients reported a higher rate of discontinuance of coffee due to negative side effects than did control subjects. A final finding that panic-disorder patients reported a correlation between their degree of caffeine intake and self-rated levels of anxiety and depression highlights the need for additional research regarding caffeine's relationship to mood (Boulenger, et al., 1984).

One elderly woman we interviewed for our program reported that she routinely drank twenty to twenty-five cups of strong tea per day, each with two teaspoons of sugar. Since she presented with reports of long-term generalized anxiety, we were surprised that she had never considered that her caffeine intake might have some bearing on her symptomatology. We were also surprised that her caffeine use had never been explored by her family physician nor had her sugar intake. What is most interesting to note is that, within three weeks of weaning herself from caffeine under a physician's supervision, this woman reported a seventy-five percent reduction in general anxiety.

As an interim treatment before comprehensive treatment begins, you can reduce or eliminate your patients' use of caffeine in coffee, tea, soda, and chocolate by educating them to the negative effects of their caffeine use. Most people are pleased to know that there is something so simple and immediate (not to mention cost-free!) within their power that can reduce their anxiety to some extent. In cases of significant caffeine intake, a program of gradual withdrawal needs to be designed.

Be aware that there is a chicken and egg paradigm here. You may not know if the caffeine generates some percentage of the anxiety, or if the caffeine is used to self-medicate the preexisting anxiety. It may also be a vicious cycle where the caffeine both calms and generates the anxiety. A good example to use when explaining this calming/stimulating quality of caffeine is that of the heavy cigarette smoker's reaction to the effects of nicotine. When introduced into the system, the nicotine's effect is calming. However, when its effect wears off, the withdrawal from the nicotine generates distress that is only immediately relieved with another cigarette (more nicotine).

11. Check for Alcohol or Other Drug Abuse as Self-medication for the Disorder.

Anxiety disorder patients seem to fall into one of two vastly different categories. Those who reach out for comprehensive treatment tend to be extremely conservative in their use of any kind of medication. They are the kind of people who need to have a headache of excruciating proportions before considering using aspirin for relief. Even then, they cut a child's aspirin in half for fear of somehow losing control while under the most minimal of chemical influence. These same patients will report that they almost never drink alcohol, and that they dislike the sensation of alcohol use of any proportion.

The opposite group of anxiety-disorder patients use chemical substances much more freely, perhaps even in an abusive way to control anxiety symptoms. This may be particularly true of men. Here, the man who has to make a sales call in the next county cannot afford to suffer the effects of panic. He reasons, "If I can't control my fear of being away from home or safety, I may lose my job. Now that is real cause for panic!" Consequently, this man may stop for a beer or two before entering a situation that is difficult for him.

Surveys conducted with alcoholic populations have reported that many alcoholics acknowledged having a panic disorder or phobic disorder that *predated* the onset of alcohol abuse (Mullaney and Trippett, 1979, Smail, et al., 1984). This information suggests that a population of panic victims attempt to self-medicate their anxiety through alcohol. In fact, many panic and phobia specialists concur that one might find as many or more male agoraphobics and male panic-disorder victims in a bar than in a treatment program. Perhaps with more and more women working outside the home, this pattern will become equalized between the sexes.

It is our experience that, for panic victims who seek help, any drug abuse is typically limited to alcohol and/or prescription drugs rather than illicit drug use. It is also our experience that these people are very aware of their use of alcohol or tranquilizers as self-medication, and are concerned that it is self-defeating. However, many also reluctantly continue this form of self-medication by reasoning that it is the lesser of two evils if their anxiety can be reduced.

As a physician, you can question whether this behavior is present by proceeding directly yet tactfully. You might ask, "Do you find yourself using anything special to help reduce your feelings of anxiety or panic?" If the response is vague, you might continue with, "Some people find that a glass or two of wine is helpful, or that they can use a prescription drug of some kind for a little relief. Does this sound like you?" It is our experience that the anxiety-disorder patient is quite open about the kinds of devices used and is willing to discuss that behavior with a caring professional.

This kind of dialogue is extremely important for three reasons:

1. it provides information to you about any substance use that may contribute to the clinical picture

2. it allows you to educate the patient about the self-defeating aspects of their drug use, and
3. it lays the foundation for your recommendation that specialized help be pursued as a more effective strategy for symptom relief

12. Learn from Your Patient about the Disorder and What They Request from a Physician.

Panic patients are a valuable source for gaining insight on the firsthand experience of panic disorder and agoraphobia. They can educate you about the thoughts, feelings, behaviors, and life-style of these disorders as well or better than the diagnostic criteria for these disorders. By asking them about their own personal experience with their disorder and what information you can offer that is most helpful to them, you can serve that patient and similar patients best.

While a lack of assertiveness is a common problem with people who develop such disorders, when asked, they will speak fully and openly about their panic experience and their needs to you. It usually just takes asking, "How can I best help you?" to elicit such valuable information.

When we surveyed panic patients who completed or are completing the TERRAP program we offer, we asked them, "How could your *physician* be most helpful to you?" Here are representative responses:

"My doctor could have helped me by knowing more about what I could do. He was nice and understanding, but he just offered me tranquilizers. If he had told me that my phobia could be worked on in therapy and that I could reach the level of recovery that I have, I would have been very relieved."

"He could understand agoraphobia better. I don't think he even knew what I had. I wish that he had told me what my symptoms were indicative of, i.e., agoraphobia, so that I would have a basis to find the right kind of help for myself."

"Give me a thorough checkup and let me know I'm fine physically. Seeing a cardiologist was one of the most reassuring things I did."

"A doctor should be up on the latest treatment methods for phobias and panic and be able to refer you to a specialist who can help."

"Be more understanding when I get upset."

"Have more time to talk to me."

"Rule out any physical problems, then put the patient in touch with the TERRAP program."

"My doctor was terrific. After directing me where to get help, he treated me as if I were normal."

* * *

As is evident here, the main requests made of the physician by the vast majority of the responses we received were: (a) screening for any medical condition generating or complicating the symptomatology, (b) education about the disorder, (c) direction to a comprehensive treatment source, (d) ongoing interest in the patient's condition demonstrated by questioning and listening, and (e) being treated as a "normal" person experiencing an emotional disorder.

13. Educate Your Local Medical Group or Society about Comprehensive Treatment Sources for these Disorders.

In speaking with physicians referring to us for the first time, they say how helpful it is to learn that there is comprehensive treatment available to their patients. Many express past frustration at diagnosing an anxiety disorder, but not knowing of referral sources for specific treatment. Consequently, they were aware that these patients often left their offices feeling more frustrated than upon entering.

By educating your colleagues to comprehensive treatment in your area, you will facilitate both diagnosis of disorders of panic and specific referral sources for treatment. You might also consider arranging a presentation by providers of such a program at one of your formal meetings. Most specialists are happy to provide more information on their programs and to answer questions on diagnosis and treatment strategies.

14. Alert Emergency Room Physicians to Comprehensive Treatment Sources for these Disorders.

The emergency room of your local hospital is a common collecting area for panic patients. Many first-time panic attacks are presented there since the victim often believes his or her health is in grave danger. It is estimated that nearly two-thirds of panic disorders progress to agoraphobia if not effectively treated. Accordingly, the emergency room physician is in the very valuable position of being able to identify a problem at a point where effective treatment is still within the realm of preventive medicine. The emergency room physician can identify the disorder, provide basic information about the disorder, and refer the patient to a treatment program able to prevent its progression to a more disabling disorder.

6

Encouragement and Advice from
Support People
and Recovered Panic Victims

There *is* a light at the end of the tunnel of this difficult but challenging time for you and your panic victim. You're skeptical, you say? That's not surprising. Unfortunately, as with many disorders, or at times of particular stress, we can doubt the existence of such a light simply because we have no contact with anyone who is living proof that such difficulties can be overcome. Harder still is finding that person whose life and mental attitude attest to the fact that we can emerge stronger and more positive from meeting such a difficult challenge. That is what this chapter is all about.

How You as a Support Person Will Change

So far, we have focused on the development and treatment of such disorders, the frustration for the victim and those who care about him, obstacles and paths to recovery, and practical advice for the main support people of the victim. Now for the encouraging part—the part that shows not only that recovery is within reach, but that both the victim and the support people can benefit from recovery in ways they never foresaw.

What is the secret to getting from the point of feeling overwhelmed by your panic victim's disorder to enjoying the rewards of recovery with that person? A simple change of gears on your part. A change from one crucial stage in your thinking to another; a transition from what we call the "BUT WHY?!" stage to the "PARTNER IN RECOVERY" stage. Unless you and other main support people of the victim make the transition from one stage to the other, energy that could be channeled into aiding the panic victim's recovery is needlessly wasted on trying to find logic in the disorder. The simple truth is that you don't *need* to find logic in the disorder. It doesn't matter *why* the victim is thinking and behaving the way he or she is. Leave the insights involving that part of the disorder to the victim. What matters from your position is that you are able to help the victim in the best way that you can, the way we have outlined in this book.

A simple analogy can make this very important point a little clearer. Suppose you're driving down a bumpy country road on your way to an important appointment. Suddenly, without warning, your car veers off the road and into a rut. As you get out of the car, you see that it's at a strange angle and that some skillful maneuvering is needed to get out of the rut.

There are basically three strategies people employ in such a situation. Some people spend a tremendous amount of energy trying to figure out *how* they got into the rut to begin with. They look at the tires, climb in and out of the rut looking for clues, and generally do several of the things many of us do when we trip and try to recover our dignity by retracing our steps to find a logical reason *why* we tripped. A second group of people approach the rut situation by loudly, perhaps profanely, bemoaning the fact that they have driven into the rut and have suffered considerable inconvenience. The third group of people in this situation are the wisest. They don't particularly care *how* they got into the rut, or how frustrating it is to *be* in the rut. What they focus all of their energy on is *getting out* of the rut! And, logically, these are the people who get out of the rut the fastest.

As a support person trying to reach a destination of recovery with your panic victim, you can squander your energy focusing on *why* he or she has this disorder. You can also squander energy on feeling frustrated or complaining about having to deal with the disorder. Both of these practices are human, understandable, and common. However, they are not practices that speed recovery. Indeed, they are practices that are obstacles to recovery in that, in this diversion of valuable energy, you are not able to become a complete partner with the panic victim in changing gears, accelerating, and getting out of the rut! You remain stuck in the "BUT WHY?!" rut.

Let's get more specific by giving examples of survey statements we received from the support people of our TERRAP members. Each one is indicative of the "BUT WHY?!" stage, and, as such, prevented the progression to the "PARTNER IN RECOVERY" stage:

"The phobia was hard for me to understand because it seemed like such an irrational kind of fear. I thought that anyone should be able to reason their way out of the situation."

"Since I have not experienced the same symptoms and phobias, it was hard to understand that one phobia can do all of the damage that it does."

"I just couldn't understand why she wasn't able to enjoy life more."

"Because shopping in malls is so easy for me, I just couldn't understand how it could be so hard for someone else."

"The hardest thing for me to understand was why one thing couldn't be pinpointed as the phobia's cause and cure. I also couldn't understand why there are so many different approaches to understanding the phobic. It made getting help for my wife very confusing."

* * *

What is the key to moving from the "BUT WHY?!" stage to the "PARTNER IN RECOVERY" stage? Education. The kind of information that comes from a comprehensive treatment program where the support people are employed as pivotal members of the treatment plan by learning simple facts that result in rechanneling energy from practices keeping the victim (and themselves) in the rut to practices that get *everybody* out of the rut. Here are examples of survey statements from our TERRAP members' support people highlighting that change of gears from the "BUT WHY?!" stage to the "PARTNER IN RECOVERY" stage:

"The most helpful thing I learned was the fact that, although the fear of the victim is irrational, it is *real*, and I needed to *deal* with it by helping my husband reach recovery."

"I learned that you have to put aside the *why* questions to deal with the reaction of what the phobic is experiencing. Once the person is stable (thinking clearly, breathing regularly, and more relaxed), then you can go back and talk about what caused the anxiety."

"I learned to be more patient and understanding and that a phobic *can* improve and deal with the fear. It was so comforting to find that there was a light at the end of the tunnel."

"I learned that this was a true phobia, and that it had to be dealt with properly and professionally. Sitting in with my phobic spouse at sessions with her therapist helped me understand the phobia and how I could best help her recover."

"I learned to let the phobic work through the panic attack, and that there is no one answer to its treatment."

"I learned that you could not force change in the panic victim. They had to do it themselves in small steps and I had to be very patient."

* * *

And now some survey statements that are representative of full-fledged partners in recovery. Use them to see the successful transition of stages and also as guidelines for practices helpful in aiding the panic victim's recovery:

"My wife was unable to enter shopping malls at all when she started treatment. With the guidance of her therapist, I learned how to separate from her while shopping after she was at the point of entering the mall. Most of all, I helped by being patient and trying to be as understanding as I could. This kept the lines of communication open between us."

"I helped by encouraging my wife in her successes, and supporting her in her setbacks. I made sure she knew I would be there should I be needed, e.g., waiting in the store, in the car, etc."

"I tried to help by not putting any pressure on her and gave encouragement for what was accomplished."

"I helped my wife by remembering the instructions given me by her therapist, reminding her how to practice, and what she should be doing, and understanding that she could stop whenever she wanted to. I reminded her that the more she practiced, the faster she could recover, and I put time aside to help her practice."

"Talking to my husband, holding him, and touching seemed to be very helpful when he was very anxious."

"Four key words: encouragement, patience, talk, and listen."

"My wife told me that the biggest help for her was in me reading the literature from her group, and in attending the family help session. She felt that my interest in helping her recovery reminded her that she was loved, which motivated her to continue with treatment."

* * *

Just as a panic victim and these victims' support people go through a wide range of emotions during the recovery process, so will you. You, as they did, will feel discouraged, skeptical, encouraged, and nearly euphoric at various times. You will feel disappointed when progress seems to be at a standstill, and amazed when progress seems so fast. These feelings and reactions are normal, to be expected, and are all part of the recovery process. Anticipating this on your part and the part of your panic victim will keep you from diverting valuable energy into trying to understand these feelings. Just accept them as part of recovery.

How the Panic Victim Will Change in Recovery

Perhaps the easiest way to show how the panic victim changes in recovery is to give examples illustrating the change in thinking that leads to and maintains recovery. The following comments are representative of responses we received in asking our TERRAP members what was most helpful for them to learn in reaching recovery:

"Remembering that being phobia-free is like chopping down a tree. It happens a little at a time. It took a long time to become phobic and it takes a long time to be phobia-free. Each chop brings relief!"

"It's up to me—I'm the only one who can make it work."

"Understanding there was a reason I was experiencing the symptoms."

"Knowing I've already experienced the worst that could happen to me."

"Use every experience as a learning tool."

"Relaxation techniques."

"Treat myself better."

"Go easy on guilt feelings."

"Remembering that this will pass if I let it, and that I'm half-full, not half-empty. Real progress comes with having some anxiety levels and seeing them through."

"Understanding that I was not alone and that I would not die during a panic attack."

"You get out of the program what you put into it—it works if you do!"

"Saying, 'What if—So what!' Not being afraid to imagine the worst—let the thoughts come and they will disappear."

"Thinking of my panic attacks like a sore throat: you may get one from time to time and you deal with it appropriately."

"No pain, no gain!"

"Rubber legs will get you there!"

"Understanding my disorder and no longer feeling like a freak."

"TERRAP's 'face the fear and the fear will disappear'."

"No big deal! What do I have to lose? Just float through it!"

"Depression is anger turned inward. Feelings will 'out' somehow. Relax! Learning that others felt exactly like me."

"Take a positive outlook on everything."

"Watching people who used to be in my stage of recovery and seeing others ahead of me."

* * *

Now imagine the kind of person who employs all of these thoughts in daily living as well as in panic and anxiety control. It sounds like a pretty nice person to be around, doesn't it? That's just what happens. Recovered panic victims like the "new" them. Their awakened feelings of enthusiasm toward themselves, their lives, and others make them delightful people to be around. The feelings of negativism and powerlessness that enveloped them before recovery began are replaced with new feelings of positive thinking and power in recovery. And those feelings benefit the lives not only of the victims, but of their families as well:

1. A mother can take her preadolescent children shopping, to the movies, and out for lunch by herself for the very first time.
2. A middle-aged father emotionally locked in a job his deceased father admired is finally able to pursue the career *he* has always wanted. He now looks forward to workdays for the first time ever, and is able to focus on strengthening his marriage and the joys of raising his children.
3. A professional young man who previously felt like "defective material" is now able to view himself positively, and to commit to marriage and the possibility of children.
4. The husband of a public figure is finally able to attend political and social events with his wife, thereby squelching rumors of marital separation fueled by his continued absences.
5. A middle-aged woman who has mourned her daughter's death for thirty years is finally able to find peace and to rechannel her energy into the living members of her family.
6. A young woman previously unable to demand more for

herself is able to leave a physically and emotionally abusive husband, thereby improving the quality of her own life as well as the lives of her children.

7. A loving wife and mother, previously housebound for years, is able to take a cross-country trip with her husband and grown children, including a walk to the edge of the Grand Canyon!

8. An agoraphobic young woman whose marriage suffered the tension of that disorder's life-style and the financial burden of one income is able to take a part-time job, help with family expenses, and enjoy social outings with or without the companionship of her husband.

9. A woman in her early fifties who previously described her marriage as fair at best, discovers a new, loving relationship with that husband whose best qualities were called into play by serving as a partner in recovery.

There are more remarkable and touching stories within this very special population of panic patients. And, of course, it is tremendously pleasing to the therapists of these people to see the effort, determination, and patience of panic victims and their support networks reach success.

You can be one of these success stories. To quote one of our patient's support people, "four key words: encouragement, patience, talk, and listen." The tools are there. It is your challenge, and the challenge of your panic victim, to use those tools in guiding your hopes and dreams to fruition. You, like others before you, may find that your "dreams" are not unreachable or unrealistic at all, but simply goals yet to be reached with effort and patience.

Suggested Readings

As we strongly recommend professionally supervised comprehensive treatment for the panic victim, the following books are suggested for use in conjunction with treatment or as a first step to seeking treatment.

Readings on Phobias, Panic, and Anxiety Disorders for the Victim, the Family, and the Professional

Peace from Nervous Suffering by Dr. Claire Weekes, Bantam Books, 1983.

This is an excellent "first" book for panic victims confused and frightened by their disorder. It has a reassuring, down-to-earth tone that is comforting to the panic victim while presenting a four-step plan to manage anxiety. The author, a physician and well-known pioneer in the treatment of phobias and other anxiety disorders presents a clear picture of the thoughts, feelings, and behaviors of the victim that help the victim realize they are not "crazy," alone, or a hopeless case. Another book by Dr. Weekes is also recommended: *Hope and Help for Your Nerves,* 1969.

Your Phobia by Manual D. Zane, M.D., and Harry Milt, American Psychiatric Press, Inc., 1984.

Dr. Manual Zane, director of the White Plains Hospital Phobia Clinic, is another pioneer in effective treatment for phobias and panic. This book is worth reading for its explanation of the major categories of phobias. While he emphasizes contextual therapy—the treatment approach that he developed—he also discusses other ideas regarding the cause and treatment of these disorders. This book also contains an excellent section on how to expose yourself gradually to feared situations, thereby providing good examples of systematic desensitization hierarchies.

Managing Your Anxiety by Christopher J. McCullough, Ph.D., and Robert Woods Mann; St. Martin's Press, 1985.

This book outlines a plan of self-help for panic and phobias. A multifaceted approach to recovery and management of general anxiety is presented with examples, exercises, questionnaires, and checklists included to help anxiety victims understand and cope with their disorder. This is a good overview of what panic victims could expect to learn in a comprehensive treatment program.

Don't Panic: Taking Control of Anxiety Attacks by R. Reid Wilson, Ph.D.; Harper and Row Publishers, 1986.

Dr. Wilson outlines a self-management and treatment program to deal with panic attacks. In his discussion on identifying the problem, he clearly outlines the different causes of panic. His strategies for gaining control include both relaxation and examination of "observer patterns" that affect panic.

Overcoming Agoraphobia: Conquering Fear of the Outside World by Alan Goldstein, Ph.D., and Barry Stainback; Viking Penguin, Inc., 1987.

This book describes a treatment approach for agoraphobia developed by Dr. Goldstein at Temple University. The steps for the self-help program are clearly defined. Special issues such as the male agoraphobic, use of medication, and the agoraphobic's family are addressed, with case histories to illustrate the recovery process. The book also includes a partial list of clinics and professionals across the country specializing in the treatment of panic and phobias.

The Anxiety Disease by David Sheehan, M.D.; Bantam Books, 1983.

This book includes information on the biological and psychological approaches to the causes and treatment of anxiety disorders. It also explains the different types of medications used to treat panic. Dr. Sheehan includes both charts and checklists to help panic victims assess their level of disability as well as a discussion on how these disorders affect the family.

Stop Running Scared by Herbert Fensterhein, Ph.D., and Jean Baer; Dell Publishing Co., Inc.; 1977.

This book discusses the treatment of agoraphobia, obsessive-compulsive disorder, and fear of flying, using numerous case histories. One of the authors, Jean Baer, was phobic herself, adding a unique perspective to their presentation.

Agoraphobia: A Clinical and Personal Account by J. Christopher Clarke and Wayne Wardman; Pergaman Press, 1985.

This book is helpful for panic victims and phobics because it is written by a recovered male agoraphobic who is also a physician. The book's focus is to present the experience of agoraphobia as well as its treatment. Helpful points are made regarding the role of the family physician and the plight of the male agoraphobic.

Additional Readings for Therapists and Physicians

Phobia: A Comprehensive Summary of Modern Treatments edited by Robert L. DuPont, M.D.; Brunner/Mazel, Inc., 1982.

This book provides a collection of articles by nationally recognized figures in the assessment and treatment of phobias and panic disorder. Discussion of related topics such as family involvement and personal issues associated with these disorders are presented along with several clinical studies.

Anxiety Disorder and Phobias: A Cognitive Perspective by Aaron T. Beck and Gary Emery with Ruth L. Greenberg; Basic Books, Inc., 1985.

This book presents a comprehensive overview of the cognitive approach to the development, assessment, and treatment of anxiety. The different components of anxiety disorders (thoughts, affect, behavior) and the interventions to produce change are addressed through clinical research and case examples.

Readings on Related Topics

Your Perfect Right: A Guide to Assertive Living by Robert E. Alberti, Ph.D., and Michael L. Simmons, Ph.D.; Impact Publishers, 1986.

Assertiveness, or rather a lack of assertiveness, is a common problem for almost all panic victims. This excellent book defines assertiveness and how it differs from both aggressive and passive behavior by using a number of interesting examples.

Don't Say Yes When You Want to Say No by Herbert

Fensterhein, Ph.D., and Jean Baer; Dell Publishing Co., 1975.

This assertiveness training guide includes an excellent discussion of how a lack of assertiveness leads to feelings of inadequacy, self-doubt, and anxiety.

How to Be An Assertive (Not Aggressive) Woman in Life, Love, and on the Job: A Total Guide to Self-Assertiveness by Jean Baer; Signet Books, 1976.

As the title indicates, this book is directed specifically toward women and the special assertiveness problems they may encounter. An assertiveness inventory allows the reader to spot assertiveness areas needing improvement. Also included is a section on female celebrities sharing their views on assertiveness and the various roles of women.

How to Be Your Own Best Friend by Mildred Newman and Bernard Berkowitz; Ballantine Books, 1971.

This short but powerful book convinces its readers that they, alone, are in control of their lives and that the ability to make change is within their power.

Feeling Good: The New Mood Therapy by David D. Burns, M.D.; a Signet Book, 1980.

Once the panic victim's anxiety is under control, some of the related concerns presented by Burns are likely to appear. These usually include feelings of low self-esteem, dealing with depression and anger, as well as handling criticism and requests from others. The author presents a clear, systematic method for examining the thoughts that generate our moods and expert advice on how to restructure those thoughts to feel better.

A New Guide to Rational Living by Albert Ellis, Ph.D., and Robert Harper, Ph.D.; Wilshire Book Company, 1975.

Ellis, a pioneer in the systematic examination of thoughts, feelings, and behavior, presents his rational emotive therapy: a strategy for changing irrational, self-defeating thoughts and behaviors by examining and restructuring beliefs and attitudes. Several case examples are helpful in explaining this valuable method.

Necessary Losses by Judith Viorst; Fawcett Gold Medal Books, 1986.

Often, the onset of panic attacks follows a loss or separation involving a loved one. Reading this book provides logic for this loss-panic connection, and helps the reader to put losses and separations into a healthy perspective. Examples from psychological theory, books, movies, and everyday life are used to emphasize important points.

Life After Life by Raymond A. Moody, M.D.; Bantam Books, 1976.

Death, the final separation from a loved one, and thoughts of our own mortality can be terrifying to address. Much of this anxiety is related to the unknowns of the death experience. This book contains reported accounts of near-death and life-after-death experiences of everyday people who have been revived from a clinical death. Their fascinating accounts can be tremendously comforting to those having difficulty dealing with death.

It Will Never Happen to Me by Claudia Black, Ph.D., M.S.W.; MAC Publishing, 1982.

Growing up with an alcoholic parent is an experience common to many people who develop panic attacks as adults. This book on Children of Alcoholic (COA) issues is written by one of the foremost writers and therapists in the treatment of COAs. She explains the importance of different family member roles and the impact of having an alcoholic parent on both the child and the child as an adult.

Children of Alcoholism: A Survivor's Manual by Judith S. Seixas and Geraldine Youcha; Crown Publishers, 1985.

This book focuses on the impact of having grown up with an alcoholic parent. A discussion of how this affects intimacy with others, marriage, parenting skills, and the relationship with the alcoholic parent is presented. Also included is a section on how to choose a therapist as well as other resources for support of the adult child of an alcoholic.

Bibliography

Alberti, R. E., and M. L. Emmons. *Your Perfect Right: A Guide to Assertive Living.* San Luis Obispo, California: Impact Publishers, 1986.

American Psychiatric Association. *Diagnostic and Statistical Manual of Mental Disorders, Third Edition, Revised.* Washington, DC, American Psychiatric Association, 1987.

Baer, J. *How to Be An Assertive (Not Aggressive) Woman in Life, Love, and on the Job: A Total Guide to Self-Assertiveness.* New York: Signet Books, 1976.

Ballenger, J., Uhde T. W., Wolff, E. A., and Post, R. M. "Unrecognized Prevalence of Panic Disorder in Primary Care, Internal Medicine and Cardiology." *American Journal of Cardiology* 60 (1987): 39J–47J.

Beck, A. T., and G. Emery, with R. L. Greenberg. *Anxiety Disorders and Phobias: A Cognitive Perspective.* New York: Basic Books, Inc., 1985.

Black, C. *It Will Never Happen to Me.* Denver, Colorado: MAC Publishing, 1982.

Boulenger, J., Uhde, T., Wolff, E., and Post, R. "Increased Sensitivity to Caffeine in Patients with Panic Disorders." *Archives of General Psychiatry* 41 (1984): 1067–71.

Burns, D. D. *Feeling Good: The New Mood Therapy.* New York: Signet Books, 1980.

Clarke, J. C., and W. Wardman. *Agoraphobia: A Clinical and Personal Account.* New York: Pergaman Press, 1985.

Cousins, N. *Anatomy of an Illness as Perceived by the Patient: Reflections on Healing and Regeneration.* New York: Norton, 1979.

Diagnostic and Statistical Manual of Mental Disorders. 3d ed. Revised. Washington, DC: American Psychiatric Association, 1987, pp. 235–53.

Dupont, R. A., ed. *Phobia: A Comprehensive Summary of Modern Treatments.* New York: Brunner/Mazel, Inc., 1982.

Ellis, A., and R. A. Harper. *A New Guide to Rational Living.* North Hollywood, California: Wilshire Book Company, 1975.

Fensterhein, H., and J. Baer. *Don't Say Yes When You Want to Say No.* New York: Dell Publishing Co., 1975.

———. *Stop Running Scared.* New York: Dell Publishing Co., 1977.

Goldstein, A., and B. Stainback. *Overcoming Agoraphobia: Conquering Fear of the Outside World.* New York: Viking Penguin, Inc., 1987.

Hardy, A. B. *Agoraphobia: Symptoms, Causes, and Treatment.* Menlo Park, California: TERRAP, Inc., 1984.

Hardy, A. B., and N. J. Flaxman. *TERRAP Program Manual.* Menlo Park, California: TSC Management Corp., 1986.

Harris, T. A. *I'm Okay—You're Okay.* New York: Avon Books, 1973.

Hollister, L. E. "A Look at the Issues: Use of Minor Tranquilizers." *Psychosomatics* 21 (1980): no. 10 (supplement).

McCullough, C. J., and R. W. Mann. *Managing Your Anxiety.* New York: St. Martin's Press, 1985.

Moody, R. A. *Life after Life.* New York: Bantam Books, 1976.

Mullaney, J. A. and C. J. Trippett. "Alcohol Dependence in Phobias: Clinical Description and Relevance." *British Journal of Psychiatry* 135 (1979): 565–73.

Newman, M., and B. Berkowitz. *How to Be Your Own Best Friend.* New York: Ballantine Books, 1971.

Seixas, J. S., and G. Youcha. *Children of Alcoholism: A Survivor's Manual.* New York: Crown Publishers, 1985.

Sheehan, D. V. *The Anxiety Disease.* New York: Bantam Books, 1983.

Smail, P., Stockwell, T., Canter, S., and Hodgson, R. "Alcohol Dependence and Phobic Anxiety States. I. A Prevalence Study." *British Journal of Psychiatry* 144 (1984): 53–57.

Uhde, T. W., and J. D. Maser, "Current Perspectives on Panic

Disorder and Agoraphobia." *Hospital and Community Psychiatry* 36 (1985): 1153–54.

Viorst, J. *Necessary Losses*. New York: Fawcett Gold Medal Books, 1986.

Weekes, C. *Hope and Help for Your Nerves*. New York: Hawthorn Books, 1969.

———. *Peace from Nervous Suffering*. New York: Bantam Books, 1983.

Wilson, R. R. *Don't Panic: Taking Control of Anxiety Attacks*. New York: Harper and Row Publishers, 1986.

Zane, M. D., and H. Milt. *Your Phobia*. Washington, DC: American Psychiatric Press, Inc., 1984.